RCA OF IT FAILED PROJECTS

By

Sudipta Malakar

ACKNOWLEDGEMENT

No task is a single man's effort. Cooperation and Coordination of various peoples at different levels go into successful implementation of this book.

There is always a sense of gratitude, which everyone expresses others for their helpful and needy services they render during difficult phases of life and to achieve the goal already set. At the outset I am thankful to the almighty that is constantly and invisibly guiding everybody and have also helped me to work on the right path.

I am son of Retired Professor (*Shri Ganesh Chandra Malakar*). I am indebted to my Father as without his support it was not possible to reach this Milestone. My loving mother (*Smt. Sikha Malakar*) always provides inspiration to me. My cute loving Son (*Master Shreyan Malakar*) is always providing me precious support at his level best.

I am very much thankful to **my parents, spouse, son and family** for their guidance which motivated me to work for the betterment of consultants by writing the book with sincerity and honesty. Without their support, this book is not possible.

I wish my sincere thanks to colleagues who helped and kept me motivated for writing this text.

Finally, I thank everyone who has directly or indirectly contributed to complete this authentic work.

PREFACE

When budgets are dwindling, deadlines passing, and tempers flaring, the usual response is to browbeat the project team and point fingers of blame. Not helpful. For these situations, what is needed is an objective process for accurately assessing what is wrong and a clear plan of action for fixing the problem.

Rescue the troubled Projects provide Program Managers, CTOs, CIOs, COOs, CEOs, Project Director, Quality Managers, project managers, executives, and customers with the answers they require. The author (Sr. Program Manager, ISO Lead auditor, Lean Six Sigma Master Black Belt) has worked with dozens of organizations in multiple industries in supporting many major fortune 500 clients (both Public and Private sector) in multiple large accounts in resuscitating numerous failing projects. This book gives practical advice on how to audit projects, analyze data, and applicable approaches and solutions for those finding themselves with a troubled project that may be over budget, running late or out of control.

Anyone who is involved with running projects needs to read his sound advice to prevent your project from getting into trouble.

Many books explain how to run a project, but only this one shows how to bring it back from the brink of disaster. And with 70% of projects failing to meet goals and 20% cancelled outright, that's essential information!

The book has been written in such a way that the concepts are explained in detail, giving adequate emphasis on real-life examples.

For decades, technology and business leaders have struggled to balance agility, reliability, automation and security, and the consequences of failure are always significant. The effective management of technology is critical for business competitiveness. High-performing organizations are 2.5 times more likely to exceed profitability, market share, and productivity goals. This handbook shows leaders how to create the cultural norms and the technical best practices necessary to maximize organizational learning, increase employee satisfaction, win in the marketplace, enhance Customer / business delight and capture new business.

"Whether you are a seasoned project manager or at the beginning of your career, this book is for you if your project is in the red." --Project Manager.com

It is said **"To err is human, to forgive divine".** Although the book is written with sincerity and honesty but in this light, I wish that the shortcomings of the book will be forgiven. At the same the author is open to any kind of constructive criticisms and suggestions for further improvement. All intelligent suggestions are welcome and the author will try their best to incorporate such in valuable suggestions in the subsequent editions of this book.

TABLE OF CONTENTS

INTRODUCTION

When budgets are dwindling, deadlines passing, and tempers flaring, the usual response is to browbeat the project team and point fingers of blame. Not helpful. For these situations, what is needed is an objective process for accurately assessing what is wrong and a clear plan of action for fixing the problem.

Rescue the troubled Projects provide Program Managers, CTOs, CIOs, COOs, CEOs, Project Director, Quality Managers, project managers, executives, and customers with the answers they require. The author (Sr. Program Manager, ISO Lead auditor, Lean Six Sigma Master Black Belt) has worked with dozens of organizations in multiple industries in supporting many major fortune 500 clients (both Public and Private sector) in multiple large accounts in resuscitating numerous failing projects. This book gives practical advice on how to audit projects, analyze data, and applicable approaches and solutions for those finding themselves with a troubled project that may be over budget, running late or out of control.

Anyone who is involved with running projects needs to read his sound advice to prevent your project from getting into trouble. In this new book, the author reveals an in-depth, start-to-finish process that includes:

> • Statistical techniques for identifying the root causes of the trouble
>
> • SAP HANA Blockchain Service

- Machine Learning in Enterprise Applications

- Improve SAP Fiori Adoption with SAP Build

- Automated testing within the ABAP programming model for SAP S/4HANA

- A Scaled-Agile Way of Building Solutions with SAP Solution Manager 7.20 – Nuts and Bolts

- Empirical analysis of RCA for Software Projects failure – Nuts and Bolts – Statistical methods

- Steps for putting projects back on track—audit the project, analyze the data, negotiate the solution, and execute the new plan

- Nearly 300 real-world examples of what works, what doesn't, and why

- Guidelines and Golden Rules for avoiding problems in subsequent projects

- Different Agile frameworks (extreme programming, SCRUM, Kanban, crystal methodologies, SAFe, dynamic software development methods, feature driven development, lean software development)

Many books explain how to run a project, but only this one shows how to bring it back from the brink of disaster. And with 70% of projects failing to meet goals and 20% cancelled outright, that's essential information!

The book has been written in such a way that the concepts are explained in detail, giving adequate emphasis on real-life examples.

"Solving a client's issue may require many complex work streams, so we set up a sprint…It's a way of getting people to

be collaborative, take accountability and feel empowered".
-- TAMARA INGRAM CHIEF
EXECUTIVE OFFICER, J. WALTER
THOMPSON COMPANY

For decades, technology and business leaders have struggled to balance agility, reliability, automation and security, and the consequences of failure are always significant. The effective management of technology is critical for business competitiveness. High-performing organizations are 2.5 times more likely to exceed profitability, market share, and productivity goals. This handbook shows leaders how to create the cultural norms and the technical best practices necessary to maximize organizational learning, increase employee satisfaction, win in the marketplace, enhance Customer / business delight and capture new business.

"Whether you are a seasoned project manager or at the beginning of your career, this book is for you if your project is in the red."
--Project Manager.com

"... lays out an insightful process, based on real world examples, to identify, prevent and recover from project failure."
--PM World Journal

Gaps . . . holes in your organization where tasks fall and failure breeds. They inhibit your ability to implement strategic plans, lead people, and run successful projects. Daily, executives, middle managers, and project managers wrestle with "the big six":

- Absence of common understanding
- Disengaged executive sponsors

- Misalignment with goals
- Poor change management
- Ineffective governance
- Lackluster leadership.

Ignoring any of these gaps will hex any strategy or project. They regularly destroy hundreds of companies' ability to turn their corporate vision into business value--taking careers with them.

Filling Execution Gaps addresses the sources of these gaps, and how to fill them. Without any one of these important functions, projects fail. Without change management, adoption suffers. Without common understanding, there is confusion. Without goals, business units, and capabilities aligned, execution falters. Without executive sponsorship, decisions languish. Too little governance allows bad things to happen, while too much governance creates overburdening bureaucracy. Without leadership at all levels of the organization, people are directionless.

1 CHAPTER 1 – RCA OF IT FAILED PROJECTS - INTRODUCTION

Definition and Impact

Troubled projects (those with a classification* of C or D) have a significant impact on Organization's profitability as well as a far-reaching negative impact on Organization's reputation for high Client satisfaction and quality service.

It is critical to the health and growth of our business portfolio to generate more business with existing clients as well as grow new clients.

Once our reputation is damaged it takes a long time to recover.

* For an explanation of root causes and ratings, read "Background and Organization of this artefact" below.

Prevention is the best cure!

Be Proactive always rather than reactive.

a) Follow the Process:

There are several things that can be done to prevent a troubled project, but one of the best ways to avoid a troubled project early on is for Proposal and project teams to understand and follow the processes and procedures defined in Organization's proprietary WWQA Process (two patents related to the Process have been issued).

b) Don't repeat history:

Another way for Organization teams to avoid troubled projects is to understand the root causes that can trigger one and apply the suggested prevention measures when a root cause is identified during the lifecycle of the opportunity. The root causes identified in this document are based on a closed-loop QA lessons learned process that analyses Project Management Reviews from troubled projects. As a result of this analysis, many lessons have been learned about the most common problems and trends that result in a troubled project. Coupled with each root cause is a set of prevention measures that has been compiled by the Worldwide Quality Assurance Knowledge Management team from their experience and expertise. The prevention measures should be considered as a means to reduce or contain the root causes - and thereby to improve project quality, profitability and Client satisfaction. This list is not intended to be a complete list of problem areas - nor an exhaustive offering of prevention measures. Experience and professional judgment should be applied to unique circumstances when determining the appropriate "measures of prevention" for any particular proposal or project.

Background and Organization of this artefact:

1.1 Process" of discovering root causes:

To better understand the flow of this document it is important to understand the QA lessons learned process. A project is first identified as troubled when it has been assigned a C or D classification as the result of a Project Management Review (PMR). The PMR reports of all troubled projects are then reviewed and analyzed, resulting in a list of the root causes that led to the project being troubled. This list of root causes for the project is then consolidated with the root causes from all troubled projects to look for trends and to rank the root causes by frequency of occurrence.

The fact that the lessons learned / root cause analysis is performed on PMR reports implies that the project is in delivery when the root causes are identified - and that is true. It does not, however, mean that all root causes occur in delivery. In fact, quite the contrary. Many of the root causes identified during the delivery phase are actually the result of actions taken (or not taken) during the design phase.

For that reason, the root causes are divided into two major sections: "Root Causes from Solution Design" and "Root Causes from Solution Delivery". Several / many of the root causes under these two categories may sound like the same root cause - and in fact many of them are. The difference is, however, that the root cause in design means that proper action or planning was not applied when the Proposal or contract was being written while the same root cause in delivery means that it was covered properly in the design phase but was not executed properly after the contract was signed and the project went into delivery.

To illustrate this, consider root cause #1208-Insufficient test plans and #5113-Insufficient testing. They may appear to be identical. But #1208 is from the design phase, meaning that we didn't plan for sufficient time and resources to perform testing during the project. #5113 on the other hand, is from the delivery phase, meaning that we didn't actually perform sufficient testing while working on the project. In some situations both root causes may apply - we didn't plan for and didn't execute sufficient testing. In other cases the design side only may apply - we didn't plan for sufficient testing, but we actually performed sufficient testing during delivery (as the result of a Project Change Request, PCR, or adjustments to the hours by the Project Manager). On other projects, however, the delivery side only may apply - we planned for sufficient testing but just didn't do it.

1.2 ROOT CAUSES: TWO MAJOR SECTIONS; SEVERAL CATEGORIES IN EACH SECTION

12.1. ROOT CAUSES FROM APPLICATION(S) SOLUTION DESIGN

1. Customer Expectations
2. Planning / Estimating
3. Requirements Issues
4. SOW / DOU Issues
5. QA Violations
6. Cross-geo Issues
7. Subcontractor Issues

12.2. ROOT CAUSES FROM APPLICATION(S) SOLUTION DELIVERY

1. Project Management
2. Resource Issues
3. Client Issues
4. Subcontractor Issues
5. Internal Organization Issues
6. No Signed Contract
7. Transition & Transformation Issues (SO)
8. Addenda Issues (SO)
9. Skills Availability Issues

For each root cause, a brief description is included along with suggested measures for prevention.

1.3 NUMBERING OF ROOT CAUSES

Each root cause is numbered, but the numbering schema has no relationship to the frequency of occurrence. The numbers are merely a four-digit number, with the first digit identifying the phase (1=Design / 5=Delivery), the second digit identifying the group within a phase, and the third / fourth digits simply being a sequential number within the group.

You may also notice several numbers are missing in sequence, e.g., 1401 or 5201. This is because on-going analysis of possible root causes has shown some to be not relevant anymore or some that are better combined with other root causes for clarity. When this occurs, these particular root causes and their numbers are removed. The root causes that remain do not change, i.e., they keep their same number.

▼**DESIGN: Possible Root Causes from Solution Design (description and prevention measures)**

1.4 SUMMARY LIST OF ROOT CAUSES IN APPLICATION SOLUTION DESIGN

1.4.1. Customer Expectations

1101. Failure to set and manage Customer Expectations

1102. Multiple contracts / work orders perceived as one

1.4.2. Planning / Estimating

1201. Fixed-price contracts for combined phases with no opportunity to refine / revise estimates / timelines

1202. Concessions during negotiations with no mitigation in terms and / or price or agreed risk acceptance and mitigation

1203. Failure to adhere to published pricing guidelines

1205. Failure to plan for risk containment via contract terms or assumptions and associated risk management plan

1206. Lack of transition plan from sales to delivery

1207. Staffing plan is inaccurate and / or level of detail is inadequate

1208. Insufficient test plans

1209. Failure to properly use an approved Organization methodology (i.e., Unified Method Framework, Team Solution Design, WWPMM, etc.)

1210. Failure to properly use intellectual capital from previous engagement(s)

1211. Client transaction volumes lower than estimated

1212. Failure to plan for issues that can arise with new and / or unproven ("first of a kind") tools or solutions

1213. Failure for involved delivery organizations to participate in the solution estimating

1214. Failure to include inflation in the pricing of a multi-year contract

1215. Failure to plan for promotion of project team member(s), leading to erosion of contract gross profit

1216. Erosion of expected contract gross profit due to unexpected cost rate increase(s)

1217. Failure to properly estimate the number of FTE hours required per week when pricing the contract

1218. Estimate not based on historical information

1219. Work estimates not validated through the use of a second estimating technique

1220. Work estimates not reviewed by a person experienced in the proposed solution

1221. Estimate based on incorrect project definition

1222. Failure to assign adequate risk contingency

1223. Illegitimate "investment pricing"

1224. Inadequate resources provided in original engagement to support RFS workload

1225. Inadequate transition & transformation plan including resources, activities, testing, schedule

1226. Client transaction volumes inaccurately estimated

1227. Inaccurate SLA estimates and /or unattainable / unrealistic SLAs

1.4.3. Requirements Issues

1301. Failure to reach common understanding of requirements or completion criteria

1302. Failure to reach understanding of the proposed solution

1303. Failure to establish appropriate contractual baseline

1304. Incomplete assumptions to bound risks, uncertainties, requirements, and / or scope

1305. No client sign-off on requirements and mutually agreed project scope

1306. Lack of involvement from the involved delivery organization(s) in solution definition / development

1307. Contract commits services that cannot be delivered by Organization within required cost & schedule constraints

1.4.4. SOW / DOU Issues

1402. Client requires penalty clauses in the SOW but we have not ensured that they are properly bounded or contained

1403. The Proposal and / or SOW is poorly constructed and lacks the specifics (e.g. detailed tasks, deliverables, milestones, completion criteria, etc.) needed to clearly define project scope and correctly set Customer Expectations

1404. Lack of DOU with other Organization organization(s)

1405. Failure to follow Foreign Currency Protection pricing delegation.

1.4.5. Quality Assurance Violations

1501. Failure to perform QA/RM reviews for initial Proposal and / or Proposal / solution changes

1.4.6. Cross-geo Issues

1601. Failure to properly plan for cross-geo contracts

1.4.7. Subcontractor Issues

1701. Poorly constructed or unauthorized subcon-tractor SOWs

1702. Lack of the alignment of the Terms & Conditions and assumptions between the client contract and the subcontractor SOW(s) which would leave Organization exposed if there are subcontractor performance issues

1703. Inaccurate understanding of subcontractor capabilities

1704. Failure to incorporate subcontractor work into the end-to-end project work plan

1.5 DETAILED DISCUSSION ON ALL ROOT CAUSES CROPPED UP DURING APPLICATION SOLUTION DESIGN

▼ **Customer Expectations (1101 - 1102)**

1101. Failure to set and manage Customer Expectations

Description:
Many problems in services projects stem from Organization's failure to meet Customer Expectations. Organization has substantial control over setting the appropriate Customer Expectations if the solution is correctly marketed and effective communications are established. Presentations or verbal comments made during the marketing phase/sales cycle, while seemingly innocent, may be perceived by a Client as a commitment by Organization and set a false expectation or be used by the Client to leverage concessions from Organization when disputes arise over scope or responsibilities.

Prevention Measures:

1. Be careful when setting Customer Expectations. Be conservative in describing a project and try to "under promise and over deliver" rather than "over promise and under deliver."

2. Caution the Client about the challenges of the project.

3. Make sure the Client fully understands and agrees with Organization's proposed solution.

4. Include experienced services delivery resources early in the discussions with the Client regarding the potential solution.

5. Do not underestimate the complexity, cost, and time required to develop and implement the solution.

6. Encourage the Client to budget for changes up-front so the Client will have the flexibility to address their changing requirements during the project without seeking additional internal funding.

7. Inform the Client of "bad news" as early as possible. Consult with experienced Organization personnel to develop a strategy to "package" the news effectively.

8. Communicate with all appropriate levels within the Client organization.

9. At the beginning of a project, document with the Client their expectations and priorities. Once the expectations and priorities are established, the project team should list actions which will be taken to

meet those expectations.

10. When appropriate, get the Client to acknowledge the risks and, if possible, agree to the contingency plan.

11. Make sure the Client fully understands the importance of their involvement and responsibilities in the project. The Client's full involvement and commitment are essential to the success of a project. The Client should think of themselves as part of a team rather than spectators. The Organization /Client team will either succeed together or fail together.

12. Conduct a formal hand-off between marketing and delivery. This would be facilitated by performing an initial Project Management Review.

13. The PM or PE should review the scope with the Client before implementation and include the Client in scope planning to identify discrepancies early (i.e., have the Client assist with the work breakdown structure).

14. Conduct Joint Application Requirement sessions (JARs) and Joint Application Development sessions (JADs), obtaining Client agreement and signoff at the completion of each activity.

15. Special Highlight – with regard to hourly contracts with committed deliverables:

   · Review the hourly nature of the SOW (e.g.; Hourly does not mean 'not to exceed') and the completion criteria with the customer.

- Set the customer's expectations that any hours listed in the SOW are only an estimate. When the contract hours have been expended the customer may either sign a Project Change Authorization (PCA) to extend the hours, or the customer can accept the deliverables as they exist and Organization's work is complete.
- Educate the customer with respect to 'estimating' hours. An estimate is a rough guess which becomes more accurate as the requirements are determined and work is performed. Estimates are only accurate when the work is complete.
- Ensure that the project schedule shows customer dependencies, milestones and task completion.
- Review 'percent of completion' and 'to complete' data frequently with the customer.
- Use frequent status reporting to summarize the project status and hours expended.
- Pursue the PCA with additional hours prior to expending the currently approved hours.

16. Meet with the customer to reset expectations. Document customer expectations and Conditions of Satisfaction in a Customer Satisfaction Management plan. Re-

solve any discrepancies.

17. Prior to contract execution, walk-through the Organization proposed solution with the customer's users to ensure there are no misunderstandings.

18. Proactively communicate with the client to review the areas of misunderstanding to ensure that there is clarity between the parties as to the nature and content of the engagement.

1102. Multiple contracts / work orders perceived as one

Description:

Organization often has multiple contracts / projects open with a single Client at a given time. Unfortunately the Client doesn't always see these as distinct and separate contracts but perceives them as one big contract. Consequently, if one project becomes troubled and has problems - the Client perceives that all projects are troubled.

Prevention Measures:

1. Set Customer Expectations early in the implementation phase.

2. Consider using the kickoff meeting as an opportunity to define separation of / from any concurrent contract.

3. During initial meetings with the Client at contract startup time it should be made clear that the effort is stand-alone and does not have any connection to other efforts currently being implemented by Organization.

4. Clearly identify and classify all Organiza-

tion contracts and existing work orders associated with the respective Client account. Determine which contracts or work orders, if any, will or could have a direct impact on your project or contract and classify these as Dependencies. These should be a part of a Dependency management plan. Clearly communicate and document these differences to the Client.

5. The Project Executive should report on each contract separately during the monthly meeting and other occasions. Each contract should have an identifiable, unique name.

6. Create individual contract billing.

7. If multiple contracts are needed, and dependencies exist, then C&N should be involved in negotiations early and the PM should be well aware of how to manage the dependencies.

8. If "multiple" PM's exist, then a DOU between them should be agreed upon and a communication plan must be established.

▼ Planning / Estimating (1201 - 1227)

1201. Fixed-price contracts for combined phases with no opportunity to refine / revise estimates / timelines

Description:

A fixed-price contract for a multiphase project may be a profitable way to structure a deal when Organization has a significant amount of successful experience with the development / implementation of a particular solution or offering. However, in cases where we do not have sufficient experience the project may be underestimated in terms of both cost and schedule. This is especially true when the fixed price covers future phases for which the requirements are not fully understood or documented, or when the input for a future phase is dependent on the deliverables from a prior phase. Unless the scope of an engagement is defined in detail with very accurate estimates (by an experienced project team), the chances that a fixed-price multiphase project will complete on-time and within budget are slim. Factors which make fixed-price contracts undesirable include:

1. lack of project team relevant experience;
2. untested components in new environment;
3. lack of detailed specifications to guide development;
4. unanticipated technical glitches;
5. multiphase projects which include requirements, design and implementation;
6. built-in conflict of interests (i.e. desire for provider to limit efforts and Client to expand scope under a fixed-price contract); and
7. not fully understanding the Client's requirements or their environment.
8. the client doesn't anticipate change as the project progresses and their requirements get further solidified.

Prevention Measures:

1. Limit fixed-price engagements to:
   - short, relatively simple projects or

phases or

- projects that have been done successfully before by the project team.

2. Large projects should be broken into logical phases with each phase bid separately, or contract for a specific number of hours instead of bidding a fixed price.

3. For large projects with no detailed design specifications, Organization should bid only the requirements validation and solution design phases (preferably time and materials).

4. Marketing efforts should be focused on level-of-effort contracts where the Client pays for the work they receive.

5. If the Client requires an estimate for the entire project a budget & planning or indicative price should be presented to the Client. These are non-binding estimates used for planning and budgeting purposes.

6. Structure the deal to put limits on the level of effort that will be devoted to certain specified tasks. If more effort is required, change control is used to obtain more Client funding. (NOTE: This requires tracking and reporting to Client the hours used on the specified level of effort tasks.)

7. If fixed price is a Client requirement or the only option, consider a pilot phase at a fixed price that will enable better estimates to be made for the full

scope.

8. The SOW should ensure the contract terms include a statement that ensures Organization will have the opportunity to validate the estimates. It should state that Organization will validate the estimates at the completion of each phase and use the PCR process to document changes in scope, price, and schedule. If we have bound our original estimate with enough specificity, we should be in a position to effectively implement change control.

9. During the engagement phase, it becomes very obvious if the initial requirements provided by the Client are detailed enough to make a reasonable estimate. In most cases, additional clarification is required. If this is the case, a two Phase approach should be presented to the Client, Phase 1 for refining and further clarifying the requirements and bounding the overall scope, Phase 2 for the implementation based on the resultant output of Phase 1.

1202. Concessions during negotiations with no mitigation in terms and/or price or agreed risk acceptance and mitigation plan

Description:

Acceptance of additional terms and conditions or increasing scope and/or responsibilities during contract negotiations without increasing the price or establishing a plan which identifies and mitigates the additional risks often causes a project to be unprofitable or less profitable than projected.

Prevention Measures:

1. Involve Organization management, Contracts & Negotiations, Legal, Quality Assurance, and/or Pricing and Delivery in the negotiation strategy sessions as needed.

2. Make it clear that Organization wants the business and is willing to negotiate a reduced scope in order to reduce the price, but also make it clear that Organization will not accept terms that make the deal unprofitable.

3. In the event that work must begin before the contract is finalized, ensure that all appropriate levels of Organization management are in agreement with the decision, that it is a calculated decision, and that an appropriate Letter of Authorization / Letter of Intent link has been signed to ensure all of Organization's costs are recovered in the event that the "contract" does not get signed. It is important to understand that Organization loses a great deal of negotiating leverage when it begins a project before the contract has been signed.

4. The PE/PM, responsible for the delivery of the proposed solution must be a key participant and have final approval/disapproval of the proposed concessions.

5. The integrated Risk Management Plan for the engagement must be updated to en-

sure that management is aware of and accepts any new risks which have been introduced during negotiations. Appropriate risk mitigation actions must be established.

1203. Failure to adhere to published pricing guidelines

Description:

During the marketing phase, Organization associates often underprice or "low-ball" the price in order to "get our foot in the Client's door". The plan in these cases is to make up the profit on a future phase or project. As a result of underpricing, projects are under financial pressure from the beginning and even minor overruns cannot be easily accommodated. Do not expect Client flexibility or sympathy in cases where Organization has underpriced a project. Clients often do not care or appreciate the fact that Organization is losing money on a particular project. They often believe Organization will make it up in some other way or on some other account. Additionally, Clients are generally unwilling to accept higher prices on later phases or projects once they have been given a lower price.

Prevention Measures:

1. Follow authorized pricing methodology and guidelines.
2. Obtain approval of authorized pricer. This is required when the estimated gross profit falls below the minimum allowed gross profit.
3. Obtain formal approval of Quality Assurance.

4. Do not reduce estimates simply to lower price. Reduce actual scope to reduce price.

5. Document the business case to support any pricing guideline deviations.

6. Obtain approvals from line management, Pricing, Legal and Quality Assurance for any pricing deviations.

1205. Failure to plan for risk containment via contract terms or assumptions and associated risk management plan

Description:

All projects involve some risks. The risks should be understood and planned for prior to beginning a project. A risk management plan which includes mitigation actions needs to be developed. Both technical and business risks should be addressed. Many risks can be avoided or reduced once they have been identified. By effectively mitigating the identified risks during the design phase, the overall contingency and the price to the Client can be reduced.

Prevention Measures:

1. Use GS Risk (the Global Services Risk Assessment tool) to help identify risk areas and develop containment actions and strategies. (GS Risk can be downloaded from the Organization Standard Software Installer (ISSI).

2. Utilize Technical, Peer and Assurance reviews to identify risks and develop containment actions and strategies.

3. Create a Risk Management Plan during the proposal preparation stage to eliminate, reduce or contain the risks. Review the plan with Quality Assurance and manage-

ment to ensure that it covers the major risks and has appropriate actions to contain them.

4. Maintain/update the Risk Management Plan throughout the life of the project.

5. For large or complex projects, conduct a Project Start Up Review / Contract Readiness Review prior to contract start to ensure that the risks identified during proposal development have been addressed by the project team and actions are being taken to address those risks.

1206. Lack of transition plan from sales to delivery

Description:

Unless a sound transition from the proposal team to the perform team takes place, much information may be lost or misunderstood with regard to the project background and Customer Expectations.

Prevention Measures:

1. Ensure that project delivery personnel are involved during the marketing process and that marketing personnel are accountable and responsible for proper transition to the delivery team.

2. For large or complex projects, conduct an initial Project Management Review, as required per the WWQA Process.

3. Upon contract award, schedule a formal transition meeting between the marketing team and the delivery team. The agenda should include:
   - Client organization & personalities

- Customer Expectations
- Alignment of expectations with the SOW
- Review verbal commitments
- Risks identified in Solution Design that apply to Delivery

1207. Staffing plan is inaccurate and/or level of detail is inadequate

Description:

During the proposal development phase plans for the skills, resources, and number of hours for each task are created. The level of detail in the staffing plan must be sufficient so that the correct skill levels, band levels, resource quantities and staffing schedules can be identified.

In many situations the skills thought necessary on a project do not actually match the skills required to deliver the project. Some of the errors in a staffing plan include: errors in the type of skill required, the timing and duration that the skills are required, and the number of resources that may be required. For example, the staffing plan calls for DB2 programmers when in reality it was C++ programmers that were needed. Another example of an inaccurate staffing plan is when we may have correctly estimated the skill needed, but we incorrectly estimated how many hours were needed or the month they were required.

Prevention Measures:

1. Use Subject Matter Experts and Project Managers to validate estimates and scope.
2. The responsible PE/PM for delivery of the solution must be involved and signoff on

the staffing plans.

3. When using GDC, confirm skills and productivity; if not satisfied, include training plan in master schedule.

4. Ensure that the detailed WBS is supported by not only the required tasks, but the required skill level, cost, task duration, and timing and dependencies.

5. TDA review and approval should scrutinize the Staffing Plan and if close to contract start date, committed names should be in place.

1208. Insufficient test plans

Description:

For many projects time for testing is required. All too often, the time allocated for testing is insufficient and/or doesn't allow for time to do follow-on testing when the first set of testing points out problems that must be addressed.

Prevention Measures:

1. Include a Pilot or Testing Phase in the SOW and include provision for subsequent Pilot/Test period as appropriate.

2. Include resource hours for the Pilot/Test phase in the pricing.

3. Include the Pilot/Test phase in the project plan and share with the Client such that schedule expectations are set.

4. Re-baseline the schedule with the Client and Organization team.

5. Have the necessary SME's conduct a Technical and Delivery Assessment (TDA) of the

Test Plan to ensure that enough time has been allocated to effectively test and re-gression test the solution.

6. The use of GS Method or other such meth-odologies should aid in defining the appro-priate Test Plans.

7. Check the IC Asset Web for Test Plans from similar projects that can be used as the baseline for the development of your pro-ject specific plan.

8. A test manager or test expert should be involved during the engagement phase to validate the viability of the proposed test-ing plans and schedules. During Delivery a test manager / expert must be assigned as a member of the project team. This test-ing resource must be factored into the cost case.

1209. Failure to properly use an approved Organization methodology (i.e., Unified Method Framework (UMF), Team Solution Design, WWPMM, etc.)

Description:

Organization has developed methodologies that are intended to help improve quality, reduce cost, and ultimately improve profitability. These methodolo-gies include intellectual capital, work products, and templates designed to reduce the amount of time necessary for project team members to deliver a pro-ject. When these methodologies are not used we are beginning with a blank piece of paper which results in higher costs and inconsistent project delivery.

Prevention Measures:

1. Provide continued education of the project management community on the merits of WWPMM and other applicable methodologies.

2. Identify lack of a methodology during Initial PMR.

3. Ensure that key members of the project team have the appropriate experience, skills and knowledge to effectively implement and execute the approved Organization methodologies such as WWPMM, Unified Method Framework and Team Solution Design. Ensure that these resources are factored into the staffing plans and cost case during the engagement delivery phase.

4. The Project Manager should select an approved methodology prior to the start of the project. This is an essential part of developing the project plan.

5. Recommend that a method expert or similar SME work with the team and review the proposal.

6. Select a methodology equivalent to project scale and contents. Don't use a complex methodology on a simple project. For example, UMF calls for many detailed work products that may not be required in a simple project.

1210. Failure to properly use intellectual capital from previous engagement(s)

Description:

Organization has captured a lot of intellectual capital from projects that have been delivered successfully. This intellectual capital can be very useful in helping a proposal team properly estimate and develop a new Work Breakdown Structure as well as to identify any potential deliverables that might be reused. As a result, the estimate will be more reliable and the profitability can be increased.

Prevention Measures:

1. Recommend that the proposal team search the ICM Asset web for intellectual capital from a similar project.
2. Minimize the modification of intellectual capital or apply no modification if possible.

1211. Client transaction volumes lower than estimated

Description:

This root cause occurs most typically in ITS projects where the project financials are transaction or incident-based, but could occur on projects in other LOBs if priced on a transaction or incident basis. In these cases the project financials are calculated based on an estimated number of transactions occurring (i.e., installing X workstations, upgrading software on X computers, etc.). By signing the contract, the Client commits to the estimated number of transactions and Organization's planned profitability is calculated on the entire number of estimated transactions occurring. When the Client fails to meet their committed number of transactions Organization is unable to invoice the Client, and consequently the profitability of the project is impacted.

Prevention Measures:

1. Ensure that each instance of the "Transac-

tion" is priced at an agreed to profit margin.

2. Use a "Tier" method of pricing. The more transactions the lower the price.

3. Do not apportion project management and project administrative time (start-up, transition, oversight, etc...) across estimated volumes. Make provision in the SOW for a minimum price for these elements regardless of volume.

4. Include minimum quantities in the SOW with penalties if minimum quantities are not realized.

5. Include a maximum number of incidents/orders that can occur within a monthly time frame. This will encourage fewer incidents/orders with larger volumes.

6. Contracts should have a "baseline evaluation" clause to validate the Client's baseline and adjust the price if the contracted level is not met.

7. Set minimum transaction baseline price in contract.

8. Include minimum volume language in the SOW to mitigate this risk.

9. Obtain approval from the executive team to proceed with the proposal if the minimum volume language is not included in a SOW.

10. Practice strict project management discipline with respect to change.

11. Ensure that Organization can terminate if the minimum volumes are not realized.

1212. Failure to plan for issues that can arise with new and /

or unproven ("first of a kind") tools or solutions

Description:

Caution must be used when the proposed solution or tools have never been used before or have never been used in the planned environment. The project estimates and schedules often don't consider the time and resources that may be needed to address any potential issues that may arise because a tool or solution doesn't perform as expected.

Prevention Measures:

1. Include a proof of concept in the SOW after which estimates can be validated and a go/no-go decision can be made.

2. Assess what will likely be the tool's level of maturity or stability at the time of planned implementation

3. Factor time in the estimates and schedules for piloting or prototyping the new solution or tool. Commit to a firm Price for the Pilot Stage and once the pilot has been successful then submit a firm price for the remainder of the project

4. Consider the addition of Subject Matter Experts to assist with the implementation.

5. Make sure that an alternative has been identified as a backup in case the proposed solution or tool does not work. Include estimates for manual rework or higher levels of manual effort that may be required in the alternate solution.

6. Include study and training plan in master schedule and examine these tool and solutions.

1213. Failure for involved delivery organizations to participate in the solution estimating

Description:

The delivery organizations are best qualified to determine if the proposed estimates are realistic so they must be included in the estimating process. Solution Design teams may have based their estimates on previous similar proposals they worked on but the delivery organizations will be able to provide the necessary insight about whether or not those estimates turned out to be accurate.

Prevention Measures:

1. The CSE or TSM should ensure that qualified SMEs from the delivery organizations work with the engagement team to develop the estimates.

2. If a delivery organization does not participate in the solution estimating, the engagement team should ensure a qualified SME from delivery reviews the estimates before the cost case is finalized.

1214. Failure to include inflation in the pricing of a multi-year contract

Description:

Inflation can be a significant issue in many countries and failure to plan for it can seriously impact the planned gross profit of a contract.

Prevention Measures:

1. Validate with the Pricier that the rules for handling the impact of inflation have been factored into the pricing case.

2. On a cross-geography engagement, the Lead Geo/IOT QA representative must ensure that the issue of inflation has been addressed in all Participating Geo's/IOT's for the duration of the contract.

3. Validate with the pricier that we have gotten a fixed-price quotation from the subcontractor, and have added inflation cost to Organization delivery cost every year at during pricing.

1215. Failure to plan for promotion of project team member(s), leading to erosion of contract gross profit

Description:

Since the performance periods of many contracts span multiple years it is possible for members of the project team to get promoted during that time. When this is not taken into consideration, the cost case will not reflect the true anticipated costs of delivering the solution. As soon as the promotions start to occur the contract's gross profit is impacted.

Prevention Measures:

1. Determine how long each key member of the project team is scheduled to remain on the contract and review the potential for a promotion to occur during that time frame.

2. Ensure that the cost case addresses the impact of any potential promotions for key members of the project team.

3. Find a more suitable role for and plan to replace the promoted team member (prior to promotion) with a similarly banded per-

son.

1216. Erosion of expected contract gross profit due to unexpected cost rate increase(s)

<u>**Description:**</u>

The pricing for a contract is based on the revenue and cost case. If the cost case is wrong and cost rate increases over the life of the contract are not included, the contract's planned GP will not be achieved.

<u>**Prevention Measures:**</u>

1. Ensure that any known cost rate increases which are anticipated to occur during the life of the contract have been addressed in the cost case and protect Organization's cost position as much as possible in the contract.

2. If the cost rate increase was not just an oversight and could not have been anticipated, consider requesting a financial re-baseline of the contract.

3. Ensure that the vendor quotes are valid for the duration of the contract. Validate this as part of change management.

1217. Failure to properly estimate the number of FTE hours required per week when pricing the contract

<u>**Description:**</u>

The standards for how many hours are worked in a week can vary by country. Estimates of the weekly FTE hours may be too low or too high. If they do not accurately reflect the real weekly work schedule, the contract's pricing case will not be based on the real cost of delivering the solution. When a significant part of the labor costs are FTE based, the failure to estimate properly can have significant impact on the contract's gross profit.

Prevention Measures:

1. As part of the Technical and Delivery Assessment (TDA), review any FTE estimates in the cost case and verify the correct number of hours per week were used in the calculations.

2. On a cross-geography engagement, the Lead Geography TSM should verify that the cost case does not assume that the FTE hours per week will be the same in all Participating Geographies.

3. Ensure that the detailed WBS is supported by not only the required tasks, but the required skill level, cost, task duration, and timing and dependencies.

1218. Estimate not based on historical information

Description:

On many of our contracts we provide the same solutions that we have provided many times in the past. Lessons Learned information that has been collected can tell us how accurate our estimates have been. For example, if a 6 month Transition is being proposed, examine prior Transitions to see if the 6 month schedule was achieved. Not taking advantage of this information contributes to the inaccurate estimating which is a key cause of financially troubled contracts.

Prevention Measures:

1. Compare the estimates for this solution against the actual costs and schedules of contracts which delivered the same solution. If the historical data does not support the estimates, revise them.
2. Review the data which is available in Lessons Learned repositories.

1219. Work estimates not validated through the use of a second estimating technique

Description:

There are many tools and techniques available to use when developing work estimates. Depending on the solution some techniques may be more appropriate than others. So the results generated by using one technique should be compared against those produced by a second technique to ensure there is consistency in the estimates.

Prevention Measures:

1. Have the estimates validated independently by an SME using a second tool or technique.

1220. Work estimates not reviewed by a person experienced in the proposed solution

Description:

When an engagement team is developing the estimates for a solution, they need to get confirmation that their estimates are correct. Estimates are based on assumptions about skill levels, learning curves, productivity, schedules, etc. There is no better way to validate those assumptions than to have the estimates reviewed by someone who has actually been involved in delivering the solution.

Prevention Measures:

1. SMEs with experience in delivering the proposed solution should review the estimates during the Technical and Delivery Assessment.

1221. Estimate based on incorrect project definition

Description:

A complete and accurate definition of project scope is critical to having a successful engagement with a client. A lack of understanding of the actual project scope will lead to incorrect estimates. An additional factor that contributes to an incorrect project definition is when the technology proposed does not provide the function required by the customer. A common analogy used with regard to identifying project definition or requirements is that of building a house. Any competent builder knows that a house has a foundation, floors, walls and a roof. Without input from the home owner as to how to customize the standard architecture to meet their needs, the risk is high that the builder will miss the mark on the estimate.

A critical component to appropriately defining a project is identifying and gathering requirements from the key stakeholders. In this example the possibilities may include the immediate family, mother in law, neighbors, or historical society requirements. There may be special needs requirements: ramps, wider doorways, railings, lower access to knobs, pulls, doors, shelving, counter tops, etc...? Identifying the key stakeholders and spending the time to identify requirements is critical.

Identification of requirements should not be done in a vacuum. Frequently one key stakeholder's requirements may conflict with, or take priority over another. Where ever possible discuss requirements and facilitate the negotiation for the final requirements with all stakeholders present.

Setting realistic expectations with the key stakeholders is another critical step in this process. Due diligence and detailed requirements gathering at the beginning of the project does not mean that there will not be changes along the way. Martha Stewart may come out with a hot new paint color, Grandma may choose to go live in the Bahamas, or new concerns regarding natural disaster risks may drive changes to the original requirements. Set the customer's expectations early and frequently that change is normal and to be expected. Explain the change management process, what 'fixed' price means, and how it could change as requirements change.

Prevention Measures:

1. Map requirements to project scope. Then map project scope definition to what is in the contract. Finally, map estimates to project scope.
2. Confirm project definition with client to ensure Customer Expectations are in synch.
3. Following client negotiations, reaffirm that requirements, scope, and estimates

are still in alignment.

4. Have a review session with the Client stakeholder to verify agreement on Scope definition

5. Include a proof of concept in the SOW.

6. Ensure that the estimates include rework that may be required if the solution technology does not provide the function required by the customer.

7. Ensure required Technical/Delivery/Quality assurance reviews are performed and recommendations are incorporated into the proposal.

8. Incorporate a due-diligence period to refine the requirements

9. Require a joint walk-through of the requirements and Organization's proposed solution with the customer prior to executing contract or in the first phase of the contract. Make sure the terms allow for re-pricing and rescheduling the project if assumptions were incorrect.

10. Propose a requirements design/validation phase to specify nonfunctional requirements with no obligation to implement a solution for a fixed price until that phase is complete.

11. If possible. include terms that allow for termination without penalty if the requirements cannot be identified and agreed to by a fixed date.

12. Encourage the customer to budget for changes up-front (perhaps up to 25 or 30% of the contract value).

13. Review baseline documents with the customer to reach agreement on what will determine whether a change is being requested.

14. Make sure the Change Management process is understood and strictly utilized

15. Ensure customer requirements are well defined

1222. Failure to assign adequate risk contingency

Description:

The purpose of assigning contingency dollars is to lessen the impact of risk items which turn into real issues for the project. Pricing guidelines define the appropriate amount of contingency based on risk rating. If those guidelines are not followed and adequate contingency is not included in the cost case, the planned profit of a contract could be jeopardized. A frequent cause of assigning inadequate risk contingency is when the engagement team thinks that just having a risk mitigation plan makes risk go away and they mistakenly think the risk rating can be reduced. Having a mitigation plan for a risk does not mitigate or eliminate a risk. QA should not reduce the risk rating until the plan is executed.

Prevention Measures:

1. Ensure all risks are identified and taken into consideration when assigning the final risk rating that is provided to Pricing.

2. Ensure that risks have actually been removed or mitigated before the risk rating is lowered.

3. Create and execute a Risk Management

plan.

1223. Illegitimate "investment pricing"

Description:

The decision about whether or not Organization will treat an engagement as an investment opportunity is a senior management decision that must be approved by Finance. The impact of such a decision on the profitability of the entire business portfolio must be understood and taken into consideration. The decision to treat an engagement as an investment opportunity cannot be made by the engagement team.

Prevention Measures:

1. Ensure the engagement team has permission from Finance to do investment pricing and that there is a documented and approved business case for the investment price. Have a letter from senior management in Finance approving the investment pricing and keep it in the contract file.
2. Ensure that the pricier has validated the pricing case.

1224. Inadequate resources provided in original engagement to support RFS workload

Description:

The amount of time and resource that is needed to process RFS requests is frequently under-estimated. If additional resource has to be added to handle the RFS workload cost will increase and the contract's GP will be impacted. Additionally, delays in processing the RFS workload because of lack of resource can be a major source of customer dissatisfaction.

Prevention Measures:

1. Ensure that the RFS process that will be used on the contract is defined and that the amount of work associated with taking each RFS request through the process is well understood.

2. Validate the anticipated volume of RFS activity, the expected response time criteria and the complexity of anticipated requests so that the workload is not under estimated.

3. Ensure that the proposed RFS workload per resource is realistic based on experience on other contracts.

4. Ensure that the RFS activity is well bounded in the contract and therefore appropriately costed in the cost case.

1225. Inadequate transition & transformation plan, including resources, activities, testing, schedule

Description:

If the Transition and Transformation phases of a contract are not planned completely and in detail, the contract will quickly experience problems which can result in financial problems that will last the life of the contract. Transition and Transformation phases should be treated as projects with their own detailed project plans.

Prevention Measures:

1. Ensure there is a detailed Transition plan and the necessary resources are in place at

contract signature so that Transition activities can start on time.

2. Ensure there is a detailed Transformation plan in place prior to the end of Transition and that resources for staffing the Transformation are in place.

3. Hold initial PMR as soon as possible after contract start and ensure schedule, skills, resources, etc. are available as planned.

1226. Client transaction volumes inaccurately estimated

Description:

A solution will be sized and costed based on the anticipated volume of transactions that will need to be processed. If the volumes are underestimated we will not have enough capacity to handle the transactions. This causes processing delays and client satisfaction issues. If the volumes are overestimated we wind up with excess capacity that unnecessarily increases the cost of our solution.

Prevention Measures:

1. Get detailed transaction volume information from the client. If the information is not available during the proposal phase, ensure there is a task included in the contract to validate the transaction volumes during Due Diligence or time early in the contract to establish contract baselines and Organization's ability to reprice.

2. Include assumptions in the proposal about transaction volumes so that if the assumptions turn out not to correct we will have a chance to re-estimate the workload.

3. Have a maximum transaction baseline defined in the contract; if the transaction volume exceeds the maximum baseline, negotiate additional payments.

4. Specify in contract that the client should issue an update to the transaction volume estimate every three months.

1227. Inaccurate SLA estimates and / or unattainable / unrealistic SLAs

Description:

Service Level Agreements (SLAs) are a contractual obligation and not attaining them results in penalties which impact contract gross profit. We have to clearly understand the delivery environment before we can establish SLA.

Prevention Measures:

1. Ensure the SLA's are based on complete and accurate information. Make sure SLA information is verified during Due Diligence or Joint Verification.

2. Don't sign up for SLAs that are unattainable (e.g. 100% attainment)

3. Don't sign up for SLAs that Organization has never been able to achieve before. Even if the cost case includes SLA penalties, failure to meet SLAs can significantly impact customer satisfaction.

4. Don't sign up for SLAs that the client has not previously achieved. During the first 6 months of the contract collect benchmark data and base the SLA commitments on that data.

5. Don't sign up for SLAs until we have data showing we can achieve them.

6. Include in the contract a joint measurement period after which SLA's will be agreed upon.

▼ Requirements Issues (1301 - 1307)

1301. Failure to reach common understanding of requirements or completion criteria

Description:

It is not uncommon for Organization's interpretation of the requirements for a project to differ from the Client's interpretation. Requirements are even interpreted differently by different people within the Client's organization. Because of the potential for varying interpretations of requirements and the impact to costs and Client satisfaction as a result of misinterpretations, it is very important that Organization have a clear and common understanding of the Client's requirements. If the contract has already been signed, resolving the misunderstanding often becomes extremely contentious when additional costs or schedule delays are involved. Disagreements as to requirements may often result in Client dissatisfaction. To address Client satisfaction, Organization may be required to deliver a more expensive solution as a result of the misinterpretation of requirements.

Prevention Measures:

1. Ensure that appropriately skilled and experienced personnel are involved in the marketing phase and proposal develop-

ment.

2. To avoid misunderstandings between Organization and the Client regarding the requirements, Organization should arrange to have a "walk-through" of the requirements.

3. The first phase of the contract could be designed as a requirements validation and solution design phase.

4. Organization should try to persuade the Client to allow Organization to validate the requirements and proposed solution with the users even if the RFP process does not specify a validation step.

5. During the marketing discussions and in the Organization cover letter and proposal, state that Organization recommends a joint walk-through of the requirements, the Statement of Work and solution description before the contract is signed.

6. Include the Client in scope planning sessions to assist with developing the work breakdown structure. Doing so will help in identification of any mismatch in Customer Expectations.

7. Requirements should not just be reviewed by the Client, they should be "approved" through a formal process before the project moves forward. It's better to address misunderstandings in the early stages of the project before the design and development activities begin.

8. Conduct fully facilitated Joint Application Requirements (JAR) and Joint Application

Development (JAD) sessions at the beginning of the project to establish the project baseline and refine the scope of work. The objective is to have the Client signoff on the requirements and design at the completion of these activities, upon which time they are frozen and any changes are subject to change control.

9. Conduct a kick-off meeting to review the project requirements in the SOW, completion criteria, confirm the Customer's Conditions of Satisfaction, and set expectations.

10. Create a detailed project plan which includes project milestones. Review milestone attainment with customer regularly.

11. For requirements that do not meet the proposed solution conduct a gap analysis to determine the scope of the problem. Propose a requirements revalidation task (via Project Change Request).

12. Develop action plans to address the issues and manage them via the project's Issues Management Process.

13. Establish and maintain Strong Project Management disciplines for the team.

14. Incorporate a review of the project schedule, status, and completion criteria into regular status meetings with the client to promote ongoing discussion using a common project baseline and schedule. Use the status reports to create a documented history and to help with early identification of issues.

1302. Failure to reach understanding of the proposed solution

Description:

There have been situations where Organization clearly understood the Client's technical requirements but Organization's solution was not **how** the Client wanted its requirements met. There are often many different approaches and technical solutions (often with significantly different costs) which meet particular requirements. Some solutions are acceptable to a Client and some are unacceptable to the Client, even though they technically meet the requirements. To avoid costly disputes, the Client should have a clear understanding of Organization's proposed solution and how it meets their requirements. If the contract has already been signed, resolving a misunderstanding often becomes extremely contentious if additional costs or schedule delays are involved.

Prevention Measures:

(These are the same prevention measures as #1301, except the focus is on the solution details rather than the requirements.)

1. Ensure that appropriately skilled and experienced personnel are involved in the marketing phase and proposal development.

2. To avoid misunderstandings between Organization and the Client regarding Organization's the proposed solution, Organization should arrange to have a "walk-through" of the proposed solution.

3. The first phase of the contract could be de-

signed as a requirements validation and solution design phase.

4. Organization should try to persuade the Client to allow Organization to validate the requirements and proposed solution with the users even if the RFP process does not specify a validation step.

5. During the marketing discussions and in the Organization cover letter and proposal, state that Organization recommends a joint walk-through of the requirements, the Statement of Work and solution description before the contract is signed.

6. Propose a JAR and JAD as separate projects. (If they are not separate projects, make sure that the work is hourly, not fixed price)

7. Ensure that appropriately skilled and experienced personnel are involved in the marketing phase and proposal development.

8. Identify and document with the customer their Conditions of Satisfaction with regard to the solution during proposal design.

9. Design the first phase of the contract as a requirements validation and solution design phase.

10. Demonstrate the value to the Customer of allowing Organization to validate the requirements and proposed solution with the users.

1303. Failure to establish appropriate contractual baseline

Description:

For ITS engagements and Systems Integration and

Application Development (SI/AD) projects, requirements documents generally serve as a poor contractual baseline. The contractual baseline forms the baseline for scope and technical project Change Management. The baselines are refined as the project progresses as the detailed WBS and project implementation plan are developed. The requirements documentation is usually too high level and the currency is not maintained and does not serve as a valid contractual baseline. A Client's documented requirements can be addressed with a variety of solutions which involve a variety of costs to deliver. Managing change and scope can be extremely difficult when the Client's requirements serve as the baseline. If the requirements serve as the technical baseline, and Organization discovers that it must develop a different solution than it originally priced, Organization has no basis to go back for a change order if the requirements have not changed. If Organization's proposed solution serves as the technical baseline and it is decided that a different solution should be implemented, Organization can then issue a change order to cover any additional costs incurred as a result of the new approach. Note, however, that if Organization has failed to describe in detail the solution that was proposed and priced, then Organization has a very weak position to establish whether a different approach is a change to the baseline. Requirements documents for Strategic Outsourcing projects work well as a baseline because Organization's wants the option of finding more efficient approaches to meet the Client's processing requirements. To the extent Organization can meet the requirements by using less costly approaches and technology, Organization usually profits.

Prevention Measures:

1. Avoid using Client requirements documents as the sole contractual baseline. Use Organization's proposed solution description in the SOW or proposal as the baseline upon which change orders will be established.

2. Client requirements documents can be used for Strategic Outsourcing projects without the same risks as SI/AD projects.

3. Organization's proposal should include a detailed solution description (not just tasks descriptions) which should serve as the baseline until the external design is developed.

4. Organization's solution description can be included in the proposal, SOW or referenced as an appendix to the SOW.

5. Unless the contract is on a time and materials basis to develop a solution based on a Client requirements document, Organization should, to the extent practical, be very careful in using a requirements document as a contractual baseline for a solution.

6. One alternative to using the requirements as a baseline is for Organization's proposal to include a detailed solution description (not just task descriptions) which could serve as the baseline until the external design is developed. The solution description should also cross-reference the requirements so the Client can understand how Organization's proposed solution ad-

dresses each requirement. Organization's solution description can be included in the proposal, SOW or referenced as an appendix to the SOW. Once the external design is developed, it (along with any approved change orders) should supersede the solution description as the baseline.

7. For RAD development, the scope should be bounded in additional ways such as maximum number of iterations or up to X amount of hours per function.

8. If Organization cannot describe the solution in detail at the inception of the contract, a Time and Materials Design Phase should be proposed. When the Design Phase is complete, Organization can then bid on the implementation phase with a clear understanding of the effort required.

9. Include all relevant assumptions in the SOW.

10. Conduct fully facilitated Joint Application Requirements (JAR) and Joint Application Development (JAD) sessions at the beginning of the project to establish the project baseline and refine the scope of work. The objective is to have the Client signoff on the requirements and design at the completion of these activities, upon which time they are frozen and any changes are subject to change control.

11. Conduct a gap analysis to determine the scope of the problem. For significant variance, conduct an immediate assessment of the problem and develop and action plan to address.

12. Consider proposing a requirements re-validation task (via Project Change Request).

13. Bring in direct involvement of an experienced technical architect to the project.

14. If appropriate, obtain the customer's agreement (via Project Change Request) of the new baseline that results from the gap analysis.

15. Establish strong Project Management disciplines for the team.

16. Ensure that contractual and configuration change management processes are established and rigorously manage changes to defined and accepted baselines.

1304. Incomplete assumptions to bound risks, uncertainties, requirements, and / or scope

Description:

If we do not document the assumptions that we made when we developed our solution and defined the scope of our proposal then it will be subject to the client's interpretation. Only when our assumptions are documented are we in a position where we can negotiate contract changes with the client when the assumptions turn out to be incorrect.

Prevention Measures:

1. Keep track of all the assumptions made by the engagement team and make sure there is a specific section in the proposal to include them.

2. Ensure that there is a process for the identification, collection, and validation of all assumptions identified in Solution Design.

3. Distinguish assumptions from responsibilities; ensure that any assumptions that can be interpreted as either Organization or client responsibilities are described as such in the SOW.

4. Include contract language that allow for change control in the event that assumptions are incorrect.

5. Include specific task completion criteria that are limited by number of hours, number of sites, or number of incidences.

6. Incorporate assumptions into task descriptions.

7. Ensure that the SOW language allows for Change Management and repricing if the assumptions prove not to be valid.

8. Validate the assumptions with the customer prior to contract signature.

9. Document assumptions which could lead to Organization's GP position being eroded

10. Ensure all assumptions not resolved before contract signing are in fact Roles and Responsibilities in the contract

1305. No client sign-off on requirements and mutually agreed project scope

Description:

It is critically important to have the client sign off on the requirements and project scope in order to prevent "scope creep" during contract delivery.

Many things can change between what is in the original proposal and what is in the final negotiated contract so having the client review the project scope and sign-off to acknowledge his agreement with it after contract negotiations are completed is key to preventing confusion and disagreements during delivery.

Prevention Measures:

1. Review detailed project scope with the customer prior to kick-off meeting. Share scope with all project team members at kick-off meeting.

2. Make sure the contract is in accordance with what was in the original proposal. Review changes with the Client and get their sign-off.

3. Don't give the Client any proposal or contract / SOW without QA and pricing approval

4. Have a project kick-off meeting as early as possible after contract signing and explain contract /SOW to stakeholders

5. Reject requirements that are not clear and concise

6. Ensure agreement between the customer and Organization on a clear and detailed requirements document

7. Do not start the project without clearly defined and agreed requirements and project scope.

1306. Lack of involvement from the involved delivery organization(s) in solution definition / development

Description:

When a solution is being developed it is critical to have the delivery organization participate in the solution design and have a sense of "ownership" about the solution since they will be responsible for implementing it. If they are not part of the design process then there can be misunderstandings between the engagement team and the delivery team about the solution scope or components which will cause problems during contract delivery.

Prevention Measures:

1. Have experienced SMEs from Delivery participate in the solution design.
2. For large, complex solutions have the E2E Delivery owner participate in the design and review of the solution.
3. Have the solution costs and schedules reviewed by Delivery SMEs who are independent from the solution design team.
4. Ensure all Technical and Delivery assurance reviews are complete and the results are documented.

1307. Contract commits services that cannot be delivered by Organization within required cost & schedule constraints

Description:

If we sign a contract that requires us to perform services at a cost or on a schedule that we know we cannot achieve, we are creating a situation that will result in a dissatisfied client and an unprofitable contract for Organization.

Prevention Measures:

1. Use experienced SMEs to validate the proposed solution can realistically be delivered within the defined schedule and cost case.

2. Identify the potential for and impact of the risk of not being able to deliver within the defined schedule and cost case.

▼ SOW / DOU Issues (1402-1405)

1402. Client requires penalty clauses in the SOW but we have not ensured that they are properly bounded or contained

Description:

In some situations a Client may request (or insist) that penalty clauses be included in an SOW. This is especially true if the Client's project is time-sensitive and they have concerns that Organization may not be able to complete the project within the required timeframe. Penalty clauses might also be requested by the Client as protection for Organization not meeting any service level agreements (SLAs) that are included in the SOW. These penalty clauses, if exercised, may negatively impact the profitability of the contract. Including penalty clauses doesn't cause the problem, but not understanding or managing them is a problem.

Prevention Measures:

1. Avoid using penalty clauses unless absolutely necessary.

2. If used, be certain that Legal and/or Contracts & Negotiations have approved them.

3. Ensure that the conditions for when a penalty clause can be exercised are clearly de-

fined and bounded.

4. If penalty clauses are requested, try to negotiate bonus clauses for early completion or above average performance.

5. If penalty clauses are used, define clearly the responsibilities and roles between the client and Organization.

1403. The Proposal and / or SOW is poorly constructed and lacks the specifics (e.g. detailed tasks, deliverables, milestones, completion criteria, etc.) needed to clearly define project scope and correctly set Customer expectations

Description:

One of the main reasons for poor quality proposals is the lack of time allocated to properly write them. Proper proposal preparation is essential to providing a high quality proposal that addresses the Client's needs and protects Organization's interests. Poor quality proposals and SOWs also result from failure to utilize the Quality Assurance reviews and peer reviews to check the quality and content of the bids. In a number of troubled projects, it was discovered that the project team failed to follow the recommendations of the Quality Assurance Reviews. Independent Quality Assurance reviews are of little value if the review recommendations are disregarded. The consequences of a poorly defined or constructed SOW are that the Project Manager has no solid basis to create a project plan and disputes over scope will arise. Unless deliverables, milestones and completion criteria are clearly defined there will be continuous debate with the client about what is or isn't in the contract.

Prevention Measures:

1. Refer to the Proposal Development Guide-book for sample proposal wording and format.

2. Decline to bid on a project if there is inadequate time to prepare a quality proposal. It is better to decline to bid, than to submit an embarrassing or unprofitable proposal.

3. Attend the Services Proposal Development Workshop (SPSW0001), available through Learning@Organization.

4. Conduct a proposal development meeting for the proposal team.

5. Consider the development of the proposal as a mini-project. Assign a proposal team leader to manage the proposal development project.

6. First create a Work Breakdown Structure (WBS) for the project and then develop the proposal based on the WBS.

7. Involve Competency Leaders/specialists in developing the solution.

8. Use peer reviews to obtain independent opinion of clarity and completeness.

9. Request independent technical reviews to validate the feasibility and ensure that nothing is overlooked or misrepresented.

10. Obtain formal Quality Assurance approval per the WWQA Process. Make sure that Quality Assurance has the time to review the final proposal documents that will go to the Client.

11. Review proposed SOW's internally with management, Quality Assurance, Finance

and Legal as appropriate before they are presented to the Client. Quality Assurance and experienced staff can identify and suggest removal or rewording of parts of a proposal which may have a negative impact to Organization. <u>Once a Client sees something that is beneficial to them in a proposal, it is very difficult to change or remove it.</u>

12. Make sure all proposals and SOW's clearly state what is in scope and what is out and include the required SOW components.

13. Make sure the Client SOW is mapped to the Subcontractor SOW obligations and assumptions.

1404. Lack of DOU with other Organization organization(s)

<u>Description</u>:

It is often necessary to use resources from more than one organization during the delivery of a project. When this occurs, one resource is the contract owner and the other organization(s) act in the role of a service provider to the contract owner - almost in a subcontract type of role. It is important to have a Document of Understanding (DOU) between the contract owning organization and each of the servicer provider organizations to ensure that everyone understands the tasks to be performed, the timeframe that the work is to be performed, how recoveries and expenses will be handled, etc. The DOU becomes the "contract" between Organization organizations in much the same way that a Subcontractor SOW is the contract between Organization and an external subcontractor. Not having a DOU almost always leads to misunderstandings, disagreements, and a breakdown in the internal Organization relationship (see also #5505: Ineffective relationship between Organization organizations).

Prevention Measures:

1. Ensure that a DOU is written and agreed to by both parties prior to the start of a contract.
2. If the tasks to be performed are dependent upon the service provider organization, the DOU should be agreed to before submitting a proposal to the Client.

1405. Failure to follow Foreign Currency Protection pricing delegation

Description:
Organization is a multinational corporation with a myriad of exposures to currency movements. On a transaction basis, when we incur a cost in a country that has a strengthening currency but have a fixed contract, our profit margins are impacted.

Prevention Measures:

1. Prier's must add additional cost to solutions which are exposed to this risk but all or some of the adder can be removed from the cost case if a foreign exchange protection clause is put in the contract.
2. Ensure the Engagement Team is working with their local pricing to identify if an exposure exists and to address it.
3. Review the PowerPoint education deck "Currency Protection in Long Term Deals - Global Technology Services" in QAC 2008001 on the WW QA database for additional information on the issues, how to

address it in deals, and whom to contact for assistance.

Reference QA Tip (🖉): Foreign Exchange (FX) Risk Pricing Protection in Long Term Global Deals

▼ QA Violations (1501)

1501. Failure to perform QA/RM reviews for initial Proposal and / or Proposal / solution changes

Description:

When projects are bid without adequate Quality Assurance reviews, Organization has failed to comply with its own Quality Assurance process. The reviews have to be conducted on an iterative basis as the solution and proposal change. Many potential problems and quality issues are identified through the Quality Assurance Proposal Review process. Based on experience with similar solutions, the Quality Assurance reviewer can offer advice on actions to take to mitigate or eliminate potential problems. Failure to follow Assurance Review recommendations is a common source of project problems.

Prevention Measures:

1. Involve client team with QA rep in Pre-Bid Consulting procedural step (link); possible benefit includes: supports "Speed to Market" through reduction, containment, and mitigation of risks -- early -- in the engagement process.

2. Follow the WWQA Process and Geography Business Rules for Proposal Assurance

which define the requirements for:
- an independent technical review,
- a local Quality Assurance or industry assurance review of the entire proposal package, including the final draft of the material to be submitted to the Client, and
- for qualifying bids, an HQ Quality Assurance Review.

3. Ensure that sufficient time is planned to allow for the reviews to take place and to incorporate recommended changes.

4. Local or Industry Assurance staff are available to help explain the proper steps and procedures which must be followed.

5. Ensure that all action items identified by Quality Assurance reviews have been closed to the satisfaction of Quality Assurance. If a recommendation is not followed, the reason for noncompliance should be documented and forwarded to line management and Quality Assurance Management. Ensure that any required management approvals are obtained.

6. The proposal team should brief its line management on the proposed project and risks identified through the proposal review process. Informed management concurrence should be obtained to proceed.

▼ Cross-geo Issues (1601)

1601. Failure to properly plan for cross-geo contracts

Description:

Many of Organization's large Clients are becoming more global. As a result we often find our projects spanning many countries and geographies. There are several ways in which cross-geo contracts can be written, but in all cases the Organization offices in the countries where work is to be performed must be involved in the development and approval of the proposal. There are many legal, human resource, tax, and other issues that must be considered - and the local country is best suited for addressing these issues.

Prevention Measures:

1. Involve Global bid managers, Tax, Export Regulations, QA, Contracts & Negotiations, Finance/Pricing, and/or Legal early in the proposal development cycle.

2. Identify each country where work is to be performed and the individuals in those countries that can provide assistance in the development of the proposal.

3. Ensure that the DOU with the lead country has been agreed to and signed by all participating countries prior to the start of a contract.

4. Reference the World Wide QA Cross Geography Opportunity Guidebook and International Engagements Reference Manual.

▼ **Subcontractor Issues (1701 - 1704)**

1701. Poorly constructed or unauthorized subcontractor SOWs

Description:
Organization has been left with little leverage when a subcontractor has been selected and committed

to the Client before Organization has established an appropriate SOW and contract with the subcontractor. Experienced subcontractors have in some instances "out-negotiated" Organization marketing and delivery personnel who attempted to structure deals without the assistance of experienced Organization contract personnel. As a result, Organization ends-up absorbing more costs than were originally intended.

The subcontractor statement of work is a critical document to have in place during the proposal design phase. While the subcontractor may not actually sign the SOW until Organization has commitment from their customer, the quality process includes validation that the subcontractor SOW appropriately supports the Organization SOW to reduce delivery risk. The risks (schedule, cost and customer satisfaction) are significant for failure to obtain an appropriate SOW with a corresponding validity date before Organization provides a proposal to the customer.

One point of confusion regarding subcontractor SOWs is between the quote that is used to support the pricing, and the SOW that defines the work, deliverables, assumptions and terms and conditions for the engagement. Procurement, which is a global organization, will issue a Purchase Order based on a quote and does not require a signed SOW but there should be a signed SOW before the subcontractor work effort commences to ensure the appropriate agreement is in place. The Opportunity Owner is responsible for ensuring that a well defined SOW is agreed to by the subcontractor and reviewed by QA, if appropriate, prior to submitting the proposal to the customer. Any changes due to negotiations with the customer are also the responsibility of the OO to negotiate with the subcontractor to ensure all changes are incorporated into the two SOWs (sub-contractor and client) before the proposal is resub-mitted. The OO should have the subcontractor SOW signed before the PO is issued. The PM should verify, during the hand-off meeting from Engagement to Delivery, that the signed subcontractor SOW exists in the Contract Master File

Prevention Measures:

1. Follow standard Organization procure-ment process.

2. Ensure Organization procurement and/or contract staff are involved prior to contacting subcontractor for discussions. Utilize the experience and guidance of the Organization procurement and/or Con-tracts & Negotiations staff.

3. Contact an Organization Resource Manager to ensure no Organization resources are available to provide the services sought from a subcontractor.

4. Determine if the subcontractor is qualified and if they have an existing Organization Subcontractor Agreement in place.

5. Make sure the subcontractor thinks you are considering other subcontractors (even if you are not seriously considering others) so the contractor will give you a competi-tive bid.

6. Make sure the subcontractor SOW is mapped to the Client SOW, terms and con-

ditions, obligations and assumptions. The Subcontractor SOW should accurately describe the work, deliverables and responsibilities.

7. All subcontractor tasks should have been priced as such and match the Organization price commitment to the customer (e.g. – hourly to hourly, fixed to fixed, etc...). Any variance between the subcontractor tasks and associated price to Organization, and the tasks that Organization has planned for that subcontractor to manage and the cost estimate for the pricing case must be resolved before the proposal is presented to the customer.

8. Billing terms and payment terms should flow appropriately based on the customer agreement (e.g. Organization should be able to bill the customer for the associated work before, or at the same time the subcontractor cost is allowed to flow to Organization).

9. Ensure that costs in our cost case for subcontractor content are supported by firm pricing commitments from and formal agreements with the subcontractor.

1702. Lack of the alignment of the terms & conditions and assumptions between the client contract and the subcontractor SOW(s) which would leave Organization exposed if there are subcontractor performance issues

Description:
Organization has been left with little leverage when a subcontractor has been selected and committed

to the Client before Organization has established an appropriate SOW and contract with the subcontractor. Experienced subcontractors have in some instances "out-negotiated" Organization marketing and delivery personnel who attempted to structure deals without the assistance of experienced Organization contract personnel. As a result, Organization ends-up absorbing more costs than were originally intended.

Prevention Measures:

1. Follow standard Organization procurement process.

2. Make sure the subcontractor SOW is mapped to the Client SOW obligations, terms and conditions, and assumptions. The Subcontractor SOW should accurately describe the work, deliverables and responsibilities.

3. All subcontractor tasks should have been priced as such and match the Organization price commitment to the customer (e.g. – hourly to hourly, fixed to fixed, etc...). Any variance between the subcontractor tasks and associated price to Organization, and the tasks that Organization has planned for that subcontractor to manage and the cost estimate for the pricing case must be resolved before the proposal is presented to the customer.

1703. Inaccurate understanding of subcontractor capabilities

Description:

Organization frequently relies on subcontractors to provide some of the skilled resources that are needed to deliver a proposed solution. Just as we must ensure that Organization resources that are used to staff a contract have the required skills we also need to ensure that any subcontractor we use has the needed skills.

Prevention Measures:

1. Work with Procurement to ensure we have an accurate understanding of the skills a subcontractor firm has and their capability to provide resources when needed.
2. Understand the track record of subcontractors being considered in performing in a similar capacity in the past.
3. Use only core suppliers identified through Procurement.

1704. Failure to incorporate subcontractor work into the end-to-end project work plan

Description:

The project plan should clearly identify both the client's and Organization's responsibilities that are required to successfully execute the contract. If we are relying on a subcontractor to perform some of the Organization-owned responsibilities, we must ensure that their tasks are incorporated into the project plan so that we have a complete view of all the project tasks and can manage them effectively.

Prevention Measures:

1. Ask subcontractors for their specific project plan related to the scope they will per-

form.

2. Review end-to-end project plan with all project team members, including subcontractors.

3. Ensure that we have built in adequate time for the management of subcontractors.

4. Have a regular meeting with subcontractor member.

5. Ask subcontractor leader to join Organization internal delivery team meeting

6. Load the Master Project Plan with resources, ownership, and dependencies.

DELIVERY: Possible Root Causes from Solution Delivery (description and prevention measures)

1.6 SUMMARY LIST OF ROOT CAUSES IN SOLUTION DELIVERY

Project Management (5101 - 5127)

5101. Ineffective project startup

Description:

The goal of project startup is to communicate the project objectives, establish roles and responsibilities and refine the project baselines to ensure that the project's participants and sponsors have a clear understanding of their roles and the project scope. Key activities include conducting internal and external kickoff meetings and establishing the PM systems and procedures to control and execute the project. An effective project startup is essential to establishing the baselines from which change is managed.

Ineffective project startup can be caused by the failure of the Organization Project Manager and Client Project Manager to review the SOW as the appropriate definition of the scope. The project participants should be aware of the project plan and their responsibilities as part of the overall project. See also #5102: Unclear / ineffective project organization.

Prevention Measures:

1. At the commencement of every project, ensure that the Organization Project Manager reviews the SOW with the Client Project Manager and obtains full concurrence regarding the tasks, Organization and Client Responsibilities, deliverables, completion criteria, change control procedures, schedule, project organization and roles, etc.

2. If any disagreements occur, ensure that marketing personnel and line management are involved to remedy the disagreement. Ensure that any resulting changes to the SOW are formally incorporated via the change control procedure before the project proceeds.

3. For large or complex contracts, conduct an initial Project Management Review per the WWQA Process.

4. Hold a Client kickoff meeting to introduce the Client and Organization team members and stakeholders to each other and to define roles and responsibilities. Use the kickoff meeting to:
   - Define scope (not develop work breakdown)
   - Identify the purpose of the project and expected output
   - Identify potential risks and preliminary plans (hold additional risk management sessions throughout the project)

ject Manager and obtains full concurrence regarding the tasks, Organization and Client Responsibilities, deliverables, completion criteria, schedule, project organization and roles, etc.

2. If any disagreements occur, ensure that marketing personnel and line management are involved to remedy the disagreement. Ensure that any resulting changes to the SOW are formally incorporated via the change management process before the project proceeds.

3. For large or complex contracts, conduct an initial Project Management Review per the WWQA Process.

4. Define the project organization along with the roles and responsibilities of each team member. The Client's staff should also clearly understand their responsibilities.

5. Define an escalation process for Organization and the Client as well as ensure there is a management communication plan.

6. Establish a joint Client/Organization "steering committee" to facilitate project oversight and decisions.

7. Hold a Client kickoff meeting to introduce the Client and Organization team members and stakeholders to each other and to define roles and responsibilities. Use the kickoff meeting to:
- Define scope (not develop work breakdown)
- Identify the purpose of the project and expected output

- Identify potential risks and preliminary plans (hold additional risk management sessions throughout the project)
- Present immediate plans for the project and describe what each project team member will be doing in the next several days.

8. Include the Client in the project planning session(s) to assist with defining the work breakdown structure. Make the project planning session different than the project kickoff meeting.

9. Ensure Contract Initiation Services (CIS) is engaged early in the contract or before signing (if imminent). CIS provides the startup expertise required to ensure an effective project start.

5104. Failure to perform QA/RM reviews during Solution Delivery

Description:

Project Management Reviews (PMRs) are sometimes not scheduled until the project is in serious trouble. By that time, it is often too late to avoid significant problems. In addition, the Project Manager's failure to follow the advice and action items from the Project Management Review reports often results in the problems continuing or becoming worse (see also #5116: Inadequate follow-up on action plans from prior reviews).

Prevention Measures:

1. Adhere to WW QA Process and Local Business Rules requirements for timing and frequency of Project Management Reviews. The PE and QA should develop a PMR

schedule contract execution and adhered to throughout the life of the contract.

2. An initial Project Management Review (PMR) conducted by experienced Quality Assurance staff can help ensure that the project begins on solid footing.

3. Ensure follow-through on action plans which result from PMRs.

4. Ensure that the project communication plan includes adequately detailed and frequent communication to the business as well as the customer, subcontractor, and delivery team. Ensure that the plan includes an escalation path to management.

5105. Lack of executive management oversight / support

Description:

Line Management in some cases does not have a good mechanism to track its respective portfolio of projects and therefore, projects often become troubled before they come to the attention of management. Management assistance is sometimes provided too late.

Prevention Measures:

1. Line management in the geographies and industries should ensure that a mechanism is in place to closely track the status of all significant projects.

2. A Project Management Review schedule should be developed and tracked in all geographies and industries to identify which projects are not being reviewed as required.

3. Close monitoring of troubled projects by

line management should be instituted.

4. Ensure that the project communication plan includes adequately detailed and frequent communication to the business as well as the customer, subcontractor, and delivery team. Ensure that the plan includes an escalation path to management. Project Executives and Project Managers should keep their line executives briefed on a frequent basis with regard to the status of all projects. The briefings should include project actuals vs. plan, risk management issues and actions as well as requests for management assistance.

5. Project Executives and Project Managers should keep their line executives briefed on a frequent basis with regard to the status of all projects. The briefings should include project actuals vs. plan, risk management issues and actions as well as requests for management assistance.

6. Adhere to the Project Management Review Schedule and communicate PMR results to line management.

7. Actively identify and quantify all Risks and Issues. For those with significant impact, ensure that there are response plans and action plans in place, respectively. Actively request specific support from management based on these plans.

8. Verify that the appropriate line management is included in the Issues Plan escalation path.

5106. Failure to implement / exercise proper change manage-

ment process

Description:

Many well intentioned project teams make changes during a project without the formality of change authorizations. Without these change authorizations, it is often difficult for Organization to defend our actions, intent or baseline when disputes arise over scope or overruns. "Defeat scope creep".

Prevention Measures:

1. Ensure the change management process is clearly defined in the SOW.

2. Encourage the Client to fund a bucket of hours dedicated for approved changes (and investigative charges). This may be anywhere from 5 to 25% of the contract value depending on the length of the contract and the number of expected changes.

3. Stress the importance of adhering to a formal, documented change management process. Following such a process is as much in the Client's interest as it is to Organization.

4. During project kickoff, walk through the change management process with the Client team.

5. Early in the project use the change management process to authorize a change which has no cost or schedule impact. The Client is much more agreeable to signing a change authorization if it does not cost them anything. By executing a no-cost change order, you and the Client will have set a precedent as to how changes must be approved.

6. Execute the change management process for every change, whether or not there is a change in cost or price. Otherwise "no cost changes" may lead to overall scope creep that will negatively impact the project at a later time.

7. Encourage the Client to participate in the change control process through the use of the Project Change Request form.

8. Ensure a Project Change Log is put in effect early to track all changes, including those that are rejected.

9. Sequentially number all changes for the sake of clarity.

10. One of the best ways to manage change is to realistically set the customer's expectations regarding the solution during proposal design, transition, and delivery.

11. Tasks that have not been incorporated into the SOW, priced, approved by the business, and approved by the customer should not be performed. Avoid gathering several small changes over a period of time in hopes of presenting only one change request to the customer. Set the customer's expectations regarding change management early in the delivery.

12. There is not just one baseline that requires Change Management. Consider the Scope baseline, Schedule baseline, and Technical baseline for example. Plan how change will be managed for all baselines. Ensure that all changes are managed through the change management process.

13. Communicate the change control procedures to vendors, internal delivery organizations, and customers during the project kickoff and enforce it throughout the life of the project.

14. Document and implement a change management plan that includes the customer, subcontractors, and internal delivery organizations.

15. Ensure that all associated costs for each change are considered in the cost case, regardless of the revenue decisions.

5107. Starting next phase prior to completing or receiving client's agreement on completion of prior phase

Description:

Starting a phase before a related preceding phase is complete is a risky decision. Much rework may be required as a result of work beginning prematurely. If the client has not agreed starting the next phase he may refuse to pay for the rework required. It has been proven time and time again that this tactic does not work.

Prevention Measures:

1. Ensure that the Project Manager plans and executes the project in a manner that does not allow a phase (or task) to start before a dependent predecessor phase has been completed.

2. Ensure that the Services Delivery Unit Management regularly assesses the status of the project and is aware (by reading status reports and attending status meetings) of any decisions to start a phase before a

prior phase has been completed.

3. For every Activity or Phase, entry and exit criteria must be documented, identifying the inputs, the outputs, and the validation process for determining if the entry / exit criteria have been met.

4. Include next phase work plan (Schedule, WBS etc.) in prior phase WBS.

5108. Continuous / constant change in scope

Description:

Everyone understands that there will nearly always be changes in scope during the life of a project. And there are usually change management processes in place to address these changes. But in some circumstances the Client makes continuous changes to the scope of a project. Sometimes these requested changes are large and have a significant impact on the project. This usually occurs when the Client didn't have a clear understanding of what they wanted or frequently change their mind about what they want. While changes can be handled through change management, constant change in scope often means rework and frustration for the project team. It can also mean that the project manager is fully occupied with understanding, documenting and issuing change authorizations that they can't focus on the actual task of managing the project.

Prevention Measures:

1. Ensure the scope and requirements are clearly identified and understood by all parties prior to starting work.

2. Be sure to incorporate the changes into the work breakdown structure and keep the

Client constantly advised of the impact of the changes on the schedule as well as the cost. By doing so, the Client will understand the impact of the excessive changes on the schedule and price.

3. Schedule impacts, solution quality and stability impacts should be the main topics of discussion with the Client PM and Executives when trying to address this issue.

4. Ensure the contract Change Management process is enforced for all requested scope changes.

5. Include the impact / cost on the total project for each change.

6. If changes are too frequent, try to establish a release plan. Create frequent releases which supply function to the Client to prevent the original plan from continuous extensions without deliverables.

5109. Lack of or inadequate hand-off from engagement to delivery

Description:

All projects should have an engagement hand-off plan to facilitate transfer of the engagement from sales/marketing (Client Solution Executive) to the account management team (Project Executive and Project Office staff). This is especially true - and CRITICAL - on big SO opportunities where the marketing and negotiations phase can take many, many months. Without an engagement hand-off plan, the account management team is often unaware of the final terms and conditions, responsibilities, tasks, deliverables, etc. of the contract and are not prepared to meet the Client's expectations or provide direction to the Organization service providers who will actually deliver the services to the Client.

Prevention Measures:

1. Ensure that an engagement hand-off plan is developed and agreed to by Organization sales/marketing and account management.

2. Ensure that the engagement hand-off meeting and formal hand-off occurs.

3. Ensure the Organization service providers are conducting their Technical Transition Meeting and beginning to prepare the detailed transition plans required to perform technical transition and transformation. Obtain lock-in on Transition cost and completion criteria.

4. Ensure Organization HR and Finance are preparing / executing the detailed transition plans required to perform the HR and Financial transition.

5. Attempt to involve the Project Executive in the Solution Design phase.

6. Attempt to continue the involvement of the Client Solution Executive in the early stages of the Solution Delivery phase.

7. Contract Initiation Services (CIS) should be engaged when the contract signing is assured to develop a list of contract deliverables (especially those which are due during the first month after signing), track changes to the original proposal made after the TDA / PBA / CBR reviews and during the contract negotiation process, and facili-

tate the Engagement Turnover Meeting.

8. Compile all updated and live documents (Contract, proposal, meeting minutes with customer and internal, and etc.) and have a hand-off meeting using them.

5110. Ineffective / insufficient financial management

Description:

One of the many tasks a project manager is responsible for is the financial management of the project. This includes reconciling labor hours, travel and other expenses, Client billings, etc. Failure to properly manage the financials often result in lost revenue or expense recoveries because the project manager is unable to validate the accuracy of Client invoices. A critical activity of financial management is reconciling plan vs actual cost and revenue streams, then analyzing and managing variances.

Prevention Measures:

1. Validate project financials on a weekly basis and correct errors immediately.

2. Validate labor and expenses billed to the Client to ensure accuracy. Correct errors immediately.

3. Review invoices with the Client to ensure they understand and are in agreement.

4. Validate that all invoices are being paid on a timely basis so that revenue can be realized for the project and an accurate gross profit can be calculated.

5. Create a financial baseline that reflects the cost and price as specified in the pricing tool that was used to price the SOW.

6. Update the financial baseline with approved Change Authorizations.

7. Track the costs and the invoices (revenue) against the approved financial baseline.

8. System generated invoices may not provide sufficient detail to satisfy the Client's Accounts Payable requirements. Therefore, establish the Client's requirements for the format for invoices at the outset of a project.

9. Review the Contract Gross Profit Report, or general ledger report, on a monthly basis to verify that costs and revenues have been appropriately recorded, and were applied under the correct accounting codes.

10. The project plans and Work Breakdown Structures should be at the level of detail to facilitate earned value measurements and tracking.

11. Provide and require education and training to all Project Leaders on financial management and control.

12. Obtain the pricing tool output, approvals, supporting cost detail, and supporting documentation for the financial baseline from the proposal leader during project transition.

13. Identify discrepancies between the approved financial baseline (plan) and the initial PM estimates (day one forecast) during project start up. Manage negative variance as an issue, create and implement corrective action plans, and communicate with management.

14. During project start up, document the financial plan and processes and review the processes with finance to ensure that the processes are complete and will work in the applicable Organization systems.

15. Ensure that financial tracking is being done at a detailed enough level to provide value during variance analysis. Summary level usually is not sufficient.

16. Perform monthly Variance Analysis against the Organization Ledgers actual attainment after the Organization Ledgers and PM actual numbers have been reconciled. Manage negative variance as an issue, create and implement corrective action plans, and communicate with management.

5111. Ineffective communications

Description:

It is critical that project managers have an effective communications plan with the Client, the project team, and Organization management. Troubled projects are often the result of simply having no regular status reporting, Client meetings, project team meetings, etc. In these situations the Client is unaware of the progress being made on a project. Without regular status reporting, the Client is also unaware of issues that may need their involvement and attention. The same can be said for Organization management. Without proper and effective communications, everyone assumes that the project is on schedule, on budget, and progressing as planned. Later, when the project is in trouble, it is too late to start trying to document all of the issues that have contributed to the project's troubled status.

Prevention Measures:

1. Develop a communications / escalation plan at the beginning of the project.

2. Ensure that regular communications and status reporting occur on a regular basis (as defined in the communications plan) with the Client, project team, and Organization management throughout the life of the project.

3. Keep the Client advised of the smallest of delays or improvements in the schedule on a weekly basis. A delay in the schedule should not be undisclosed to the Client on the premise that "it can be made up" without the need for the Client to know.

4. Project Governance must be established at the start of the project and documented either in a separate document or as part of the PMP. This establishes the baseline for the majority of the project communications and how the project will be managed on a day to day basis. This also helps reduce some learning curve time as new project members join the team.

5112. Ineffective staffing plans

Description:

It is important that staffing plans be accurate and complete. A well-defined staffing plan enables the project manager to know what skills will be needed on a project and for how long. Without an effective staffing plan, the project manager is often unable to obtain the right skills at the right time.

Prevention Measures:

1. Ensure that a staffing plan is developed prior to the start of a project.

2. Work with the appropriate Resource Deployment Managers (RDMs) or other staffing personnel to make them aware of what skills will be needed and when.

3. Until a project plan can be created, use the estimates that were used in the pricing tool to determine initial resource requirements for the staffing plan. Once the project plan is created, use it to validate and update the resource plan. The project plan will determine not only the number of resources and skills required, but will also indicate when the resources will be required.

4. A project should always be staffed with resources that possess the appropriate skills, experience and knowledge to "jump start" the project and ensure successful delivery. Ineffective staffing plans are mainly a direct result of the engagement team trying to staff the project with less expensive / lower band level resources in order to lower the cost.

5. Ensure a project plan is developed and used throughout the project life. This will ensure all tasks are staffed and any deficiencies are made visible at the earliest point in time.

5113. Insufficient testing

Description:

Testing is usually included in the project management plan/schedule when appropriate. All too often, however, the amount of time is underestimated or is reduced in an effort to cut project costs. Testing for rework is often underestimated as well.

Prevention Measures:

1. Ensure that subject matter experts participate in the development of the testing estimates.

2. Ensure that "superstar" estimating doesn't influence the amount of testing needed. Superstar estimating occurs when a highly skilled expert with many years of experience provides an estimate that can't be achieved by the less experienced practitioners that will be performing the work on the project.

3. Assign a Test Manager / Expert to the project.

5115. Lack of or inadequate project management plan / schedule

Description:
A current project management plan/schedule is one of the fundamentals of good project management. Not having a current schedule results in the project manager being unaware of what tasks are due, what work has been completed, what work remains to be done, how many hours have been spent on a task, etc. Failure to maintain a project management schedule nearly always results in a troubled project.

Prevention Measures:

1. Ensure that a current project management plan/schedule was developed prior to the start of the project and that it is kept current throughout the life of the project.

2. Ensure that the Project Manager has the skills to create a project plan using a project planning tool such as Microsoft Project.

3. Ensure that the project has assigned an experienced Project Administrator, preferably a Jr. PM, to assist the PM in the PM plan development, scheduling and tracking. Individuals in this role should have an in-depth knowledge in the use of whatever PM tool that will be used on the project.

4. A contract which has multiple, related and/or dependent projects and phases requires an additional level of planning. An integrated plan for the entire group is required to ensure any dependencies are met. Client and subcontractor plans should be included. The integrated plan can be used to manage the project.

5116. Inadequate follow-up on action plans from prior review(s)

Description:
Failure by the Project Manager to follow the advice and action items from the Project Management Review reports often results in the problems continuing or becoming worse.

Prevention Measures:

1. Ensure that an action plan is developed to address the findings and recommendations

identified during a Project Management Review.

2. Assign each of the action items to the appropriate person for completion and identify a due date for each.

3. Monitor the action plan to validate that the action items are being completed.

4. Report the status of the action items, as appropriate, between PMRs and prior to the next PMR.

5. Make the action plan part of the internal status report to line management and executives, and report the status of the action items in each report.

6. The responsible Delivery Exec must provided the management oversight to ensure that the action plans are addressed, providing whatever executive support to the PM that is necessary to complete the identified actions.

5117. Not properly using approved Organization methodology (i.e., Unified Method Framework, Team Solution Design, WWPMM, etc.)

Description:

A Project Management Methodology tells you what you have to do to successfully manage any project from beginning to end. It's a repeatable process that can help guide the project in the right direction and keep it on track. On occasion, when the project goes off track, it can be used to efficiently identify the root cause and best likely resolution. This gets the project back on track in a faster, more controlled manner. The value of project management is to use a Project Management Methodology to lend control to a project ensuring the most optimum outcome, a satisfied customer, and continued business opportunity in that account.

Organization has been a project based enterprise since 1996. Organization's Project Management Methodology is documented in the Corporate Practice C-P 0-0145-030. The Organization World Wide Project Management Methodology (WWPMM) is based on the Corporate Practice. Each division then elaborates the Organization PM practice into their PM policy. This may include division specific business requirements that are included in the specific division policy. The PM then further tailors the LOB methodology for their specific contractual obligation. While the specifics may change, the requirement for the use of the PM elements in the Corporate Practice does not change.

Equate the PM Methodology to the analogy of the use of a map when planning a cross country trip. Organization has required all employees to use a map. They've gone as far as to publish the map they want used. Each division may add to the map, or place usage requirements on the use of the map (e.g. – no Mountain passes may be used between October and May). The project manager is then expected to take that map and plan their trip from point A to point B based on the contractual agreement with the customer. Many things will determine exactly how the map is used for that specific trip, but the use of a well planned and documented map for that project is not negotiable. The Methodology is flexible and scalable for any project.

Organization has spent a great deal of time and

money developing various methodologies for project management (WWPMM and PMP) and for technical delivery (Unified Method Framework). These methodologies contain valuable information, work products, templates, etc. designed to help project teams improve efficiency and profitability on a project. Using these methodologies also creates a level of consistency between projects so that project team members are able to move between projects more easily. Not using one of the approved methodologies generally results in a "reinventing the wheel" and "starting from scratch" environment.

Prevention Measures:

1. Ensure that one of the approved Organization project management methodologies (WWPMM or PgMS) is being used on the project.

2. Ensure that Unified Method Framework is being used as the technical delivery methodology on the project.

3. Ensure that key members of the project team have the appropriate experience, skills and knowledge to effectively implement and execute the approved Organization methodologies such as WWPMM and Unified Method Framework. Ensure that these resources are factored into the staffing plans and cost case during the engagement delivery phase.

4. Review the Organization Policy for Program and Project Management

5. Review the World Wide Project Management Method (WWPMM)

6. Schedule a Project Management Review to help assess the situation. Aggressively implement an action plan to address the project control issues raised during the review and schedule a follow-up PMR.

7. An experienced project manager should be assigned to either manage the project or mentor the project manager and monitor the status of the project.

8. An experienced PM should help get the project started including establishing project controls and a project plan.

9. Consider augmenting the project team with project administration skills.

10. Schedule frequent oversight reviews by management and QA to review the status.

5118. Lack of, inadequate, or ineffectively staffed / implemented Risk Management Plan

Description:

A risk management plan, including mitigation actions, should be prepared prior to the beginning of the project as part of the proposal development. Once the project is in delivery, the risk management plan should be updated and maintained throughout the life of the engagement. This helps project managers and management be aware of new risks that arise so that they can be closely monitored and managed appropriately. Failure to have a current risk management plan can leave Organization unprepared to address issues in a timely manner.

Prevention Measures:

1. Use the GS Risk tool to create a risk management plan during the proposal develop-

ment cycle.

2. Update and maintain the risk management plan throughout the life of the project.

3. Ensure there is adequate resource assigned to maintain the plan, monitor the status of risk mitigation actions and provide a risk summary to executive management. If it is required by Management Directive, ensure the role of the Risk Manager is staffed.

4. Include the Client in the risk management sessions where appropriate. Clients are usually far more aware of the types and frequencies of risk that can affect their line of business. This also helps in the Client accepting their responsibilities as far as risk response.

5. When developing the Risk Management Plan, include the specific risk items related this contract. Don't just limit the risks to those that are generated by the GS Risk tool. Make sure the delivery team understands the specific risks.

6. Evaluate the reasons that the control is not effectively implemented and develop an action plan to address.

7. Review the Organization Policy for Programs and Project Management.

5119. Lack of or inadequate plan to submit and / or reuse intellectual capital

Description:

The inventory of intellectual capital available to project teams to be used on projects is one of Organization's greatest assets. This inventory, however, is only valuable if it is collected and then reused successfully on future projects. It is important that Organization project teams have a plan to submit new intellectual capital to the ICM Asset web as part of their project tasks and that they also have a plan to reuse existing intellectual capital in order to reduce development time and cost.

Prevention Measures:

1. Maintain / update a plan to submit and reuse intellectual capital during the delivery of every project.

5120. Lack of or inadequate Quality Management Plan

Description:

As soon as Quality Assurance gets involved in an opportunity, the required WW QA reviews (PBC, TDA, PBA, CBR) and Executive Management Reviews must be identified. A Quality Management Plan needs to be put in place to ensure that they can happen in a timely manner that coincides with the proposal development schedule. If the plan is not in place there is risk that the reviews will not take place or that they will not be complete because adequate time was not factored into the schedule. The plan must be more than just a review schedule. It should identify when documentation needs to be provided to the review team so that the review can be thorough and complete. It should also include adequate time to review the key risks with Executive Management.

It is especially important that the Quality Management Plan be in place for Cross-Geo opportunities where review activities in multiple IOTs may have to be coordinated.

There is a template for the Quality Plan in the QAWB so

that the plan can be documented and stored with the Opportunity.

Prevention Measures:

1. The QA rep must work with the Engagement Team Lead to ensure the Quality Management Plan is developed and that the proposal team is aware of the QA review schedule, when the documentation for the reviews must be provided to QA, and who must participate in the reviews.

2. The Quality Management Plan should ensure that an Executive Management risk review is part of the proposal development schedule.

5121. Lack of adherence to deliverable reviews and formal acceptance disciplines

Description:

Deliverables are a critical contractual obligation. Failure to produce client approved deliverables on schedule is a major source of late payments and/or penalties. A contract must have detailed procedures for how and when deliverables will be reviewed and how we will obtain client sign-off on them. If these procedures are not documented and adhered to we

Prevention Measures:

1. Ensure there is a Project Management Process defined for Deliverables Management which has been reviewed and agreed to by the client.

2. If the client does not adhere to the deliverables review schedule or the formal acceptance procedures, escalate the problem

promptly since it can negatively impact the entire project schedule and our ability to collect payment for the work we have done.

3. Ensure that we are contractually protected from any penalties, for example, missed milestones, incurred as a result of client delays.

4. Specify the deliverable review is the client's responsibility in the SRM

5122. Ineffective management of Customer expectations on an on-going basis

Description:
Just fulfilling our contractual obligations does not mean that we will meet our client's expectations. Besides meeting SLA performance commitments and milestone schedules the client may also be looking for Organization to be a proactive partner in proposing innovative ideas to improve IT performance and lower costs. We need to maintain an on-going dialogue with the client to ensure we are ready to address their changing expectations.

Prevention Measures:

1. Include in your end-to-end project plan specific customer meetings to initially set its expectations and later to follow-up on attainment.

2. Utilize the Set-Met or other objective-setting process as a vehicle for on-going dialog.

3. Consider building into the contract time for a Solution Architect or other SME

whose responsibility it will be to bring innovation to the client.

4. Define regular meeting with the client and confirm client expectation

5. Interview the client (and complete the Interim Client Health Check (ICHC) if required by business rules) during each PMR. These periodic meetings with the client help to verify that his expectations still match what it is the contract.

5123. Ineffective management of subcontractors and their deliverables

Description:

When we hire a subcontractor to perform some of the Organization tasks in a contract we can't just assume that the subcontractor will meet their commitments and schedules and produce quality deliverables. In the client's view, those tasks are still Organization responsibilities and if the subcontractor does not perform the client views that as an Organization failure. Subcontractors have to be managed just like internal Organization resources who are working on the contract.

Prevention Measures:

1. Include in your end-to-end project plan specific meetings with the subcontractors to review the status of the activities in their plans.

2. Don't accept the deliverables of the subcontractor without review.

3. Confirm the status of the deliverables at regular meetings. Review progress, quality

and issues.

4. Ensure that a complete Subcontractor Management plan is in place.

5. Communicate subcontractor responsibilities and track attainment against those responsibilities.

6. Ensure that cost estimates include sufficient time for subcontractor management. This time should be incremented for each additional subcontractor on the project.

5124. No periodic reassessment of original estimate throughout project delivery

Description:

During contract delivery we need to know if the estimates that were developed during Solution Design accurately portray the effort that is required to deliver the solution. Frequently, as contract delivery is in progress the estimates change as we gain a better understanding of the solution or as the result of issues that may arise (e.g. resources shortages, unexpected issues with the technical solution, missed SLAs, etc.). To ensure that we have an accurate view of what the real required effort and cost of delivery is we should periodically reassess the estimates.

Prevention Measures:

1. Compare project execution against initial project plan in order to identify gaps that will help you to update estimations for the coming activities.

2. Unless fixed price contract, negotiate with customer to adjust financials initially based just in estimations.

3. Confirm them at each PMR

4. Practice variance analysis and financial discipline.

5. Ensure that a complete financial management plan is in place.

5125. Ineffective implementation of RFS tools, process, and staffing

Description:

We can't assume we will be able to satisfactorily handle RFS just because we define a process, assign some resources the requests and install tools to manage the workflow. We must ensure that the process is effectively implemented so that the RFS backlog is handled in an efficient and timely manner and that we have qualified resources in place to review each RFS so that our estimates are accurate. Lack of an effective RFS process is one of the leading causes of client dissatisfaction.

Prevention Measures:

1. Include in the agenda for some of periodic project team meetings specific subjects to review statistics and service levels related to RFS.

2. Include RFS Staff's cost in Pricing case

5126. Ineffective project office staffing

Description:

To have a smooth running contract you need to have a project office that is well-organized and appropriately staffed. The project office must have enough resource with the skills and experience to ensure that the project management processes are being effectively executed. Without the support of an effective project office team, the PE/PM will have difficulty managing the schedules, financials, deliverables, communications, etc. which are critical to well run contract.

Prevention Measures:

1. Meet with the candidates for Project Office and make sure they have the skills required for the project.
2. Including PO staff's cost in pricing case

5127. Incomplete &/or ineffective project office management system to cover key program management disciplines

Description:

The project office management system that is put in place must provide the support needed to have a well run contract. A management procedure must be defined for each program area such as Deliverables, Change Management, Issue Management, Governance, Communications, etc. There must be clearly defined processes and procedures in place to mange all aspects of the contract during delivery.

Prevention Measures:

1. Make use of previous experience and CIS support to put in place the adequate processes and procedures to run the project office.
2. Review the PM Methodology and implement a complete PM System.

Resource Issues (5202 - 5205)

5202. Lack of management of unplanned turnover of key project team members.

Description:
If unplanned staff turnover occurs and a plan is not put in place to address it promptly, cost and schedule overruns occur because of delays caused by the time required to locate replacements, actually make them available to work, and bring them up to speed on the specifics of the project.

Prevention Measures:
1. Ensure that the Organization Project Manager has a "succession plan" in place for key project team members in the event that they leave the project for personal or business reasons. This plan should include the identification of potential replacements with comparable experience/expertise along with the manner in which a transition of responsibilities from the original person to the replacement might take place.

2. Ensure that the Organization Project Manager practices "cross-training" so that in the event a key project team member leaves the project, an existing peer on the project could at least temporarily handle the responsibilities until a permanent replacement is brought in. This can help keep disruption minimized.

3. As part of the project Resource Management plan, make sure each team member's roles and responsibilities are defined and updated accordingly. Doing so will make it easier when communicating the need for a replacement from a resource deployment manager.

4. Ensure that the common processes and work products are documented and located in an Organization accessible repository.

5203. Lack of management of unplanned changes in band level for key project team member(s).

Description:

If the band levels of key personnel rise during the execution of the contract the associated costs will negatively impact the contract's profit margins. Lack of planning for anticipated increases in band levels and/or not properly managing them when they occur will result in challenges to achieving a contracts financial goals.

Prevention Measures:

1. Ensure that any anticipated increases in the band levels of key project team members are factored into the cost case.
2. If the cost case cannot afford the increased costs associated with higher band levels, ensure there is a plan in place to replace key project personnel with a minimum of impact to the satisfactory performance of our contract responsibilities.

5204. Inability staff at band levels specified in the price case

Description:

Not staffing a contract with resources who are at the band levels specified in the cost case can result in several different problems. If we staff at band levels higher than what was planned, we will negatively impact the profit margins of the contract. If we staff at band levels lower than what was planned, we risk using personnel who skills are not at the level needed to get the job done.

Prevention Measures:

1. Get confirmation of resource band levels from the Delivery manager during the IPMR.
2. Compare using Organization resources to using equivalent subcontractor resource.
3. Identify the negative variances and manage through the Issues Management plan.
4. Consider the use of lower banded resources where possible to counter the negative impact.
5. Augment the resources with subcontractors.

5205. Resource performance issues not addressed
Description:

Performance problems with resources can be a significant cause of client dissatisfaction and poor team morale. If the resources who are assigned to the contract are not fulfilling their responsibilities Organization's ability to deliver will be impacted. Performance issues should be addressed as soon as they are recognized - whether the problem is with the Organization delivery team or with client personnel.

Prevention Measures:

1. Schedule periodic private meetings with project team members to understand team

morale and fulfillment of their responsibilities as planned.

2. Define the resource responsibilities, track and monitor closely.

3. Discuss concerns with the Delivery Manager and consider an improvement plan.

4. Transition the resource off the project if the prior recommendations are unsuccessful.

Client Issues (5301-5309)

5301. Unfulfilled Client responsibilities

Description:

In some cases, the Client does not have the resources, skills, infrastructure or time to support the implementation of Organization's proposed solution. As a result, the project falls behind schedule, Organization may be required to assume Client responsibilities and/or the project may not proceed as planned. Do not assume that just because the SOW clearly states the Client Responsibilities, that the Client has the skills or resource availability to meet those responsibilities.

Prevention Measures:

1. A readiness assessment should be conducted with the Client prior to bidding a significant project. Elements to be assessed should include:

- executive commitment to the solution;
- user and management commitment to the solution;
- adequate funding to cover all internal as well as external costs;

- internal resource skill level and availability;
- adequate infrastructure to support the new solution;
- business process change requirements and adequate time to implement necessary changes; and
- conflicts with busy seasons which may affect internal resource availability.

2. Share the results with the Client and attempt to develop an action plan to address any identified concerns.

3. At the commencement of every project, ensure that the Organization Project Manager reviews the SOW with the Client Project Manager and obtains full concurrence regarding the tasks, Organization and Client responsibilities, deliverables, completion criteria, schedule, project organization and roles, etc.

4. Require the Client to report status on its responsibilities to help ensure project stays on track.

5. Include the Client in the project planning sessions to help create the work breakdown structure. Here the Client's specific tasks will be identified and it will assist the Client in knowing their responsibilities as well as requiring them to assign resources to tasks. In turn, this will help the Client determine the workload for their resources.

6. Create a proposal for Organization or a subcontractor to perform the work for the Client. In some cases this may be enough to

make the Client realize the need to take action.

7. Propose to charge the Client for Organization time lost due to Client delays.

8. Discuss the situation with the customer project manager. Follow-up with a letter documenting Organization's concerns.

9. Include and track the ownership and dependencies in the project schedule plan.

10. In the weekly status reports, document the status of whether the customer's responsibilities are being met and which ones are not.

11. Include in the status reports an issue list describing the impact of the customer not meeting its responsibilities.

12. Consider issuing a change order which specifies the impact to the project and the costs of the customer not meeting their responsibilities.

13. If the issue is not resolved promptly, escalate the issue within Organization and the customer management chain.

5302. Client unprepared to support the new system

Description:

Clients are sometimes resistant to accepting a system if their staff is unable to effectively support it. As a result, they keep Organization on-site to support the new system by delaying acceptance.

Prevention Measures:

1. Include the appropriate level of training tasks to enable the Client to support the

system in the SOW.

2. Include a post implementation support task to keep the system running while the Client's personnel become trained to support the system.

3. Include specific completion criteria in the SOW and in the project plan. Maintain Client's focus on the project completion right from the beginning of the project.

5303. Client represented by Third Party

Description:

Some Clients choose to use a third party vendor to negotiate their services contracts. These third parties are given the mission of choosing a vendor to deliver a particular project - usually awarding the contract to the vendor that can deliver the project for the lowest cost. These third parties are also given the responsibility to negotiate terms and conditions of the contract. Unfortunately, the vendors (including Organization) usually don't have any direct contact or involvement with the Client. This makes it extremely difficult to fully understand the requirements that we are being asked to bid on - or to help the Client understand why the value Organization can bring may be worth a higher price than our competitors.

Prevention Measures:

1. Determine first if award is based on price alone. If so, be very specific in what is not included in the SOW and document all assumptions in the SOW.

2. Be sure not to price in any product or service that is not explicitly required

3. Implement Change Management at the first opportunity.

4. In the event that Organization is the Prime, request and validate the viability of the 3rd party's detailed project plans and schedules and how they integrate into the overall Organization solution. Highlight and escalate to the Client any issues and areas that require further clarification as to the scope of the 3rd party effort, as soon as possible and seek resolution.

5. Contact other proposal leads who have had experience with the third party to develop a plan for addressing the third party's requirements.

5304. Change in Client management team

Description:

Occasionally there are changes in the Client's management team which can impact the success of project. This usually is the result of the new management wanting to evaluate all open projects and modify their scope to address the business issues that they want to address. It may even mean the termination of a project.

Prevention Measures:

1. Ensure appropriate language is incorporated into the SOW to protect Organization from delays outside of Organization's control.

2. Ensure appropriate language is incorporated into the SOW to protect Organization from early termination.

3. The signed contract should have prece-

dence, regardless of any changes to the Client management team. In the event that changes are requested from the new management team, the normal Change Control process is in effect.

4. The Project Executive should contact new management to determine their business objectives and strategy.

5. Develop an Organization response or proposal which meets the requirements of new management.

5305. Ineffective relationship between Organization and the Client

Description:

A troubled project can result from an ineffective relationship between Organization and the Client. Conversely, an ineffective relationship is often the result of a troubled project. In some situations a Client chooses Organization for a project even though Organization is not their "vendor of choice". Or the decision to use Organization was not the Client project sponsor's choice. In these situations the Client is often difficult to work with and can even try to "sabotage" the project. This obviously has a negative impact on the project's success.

There are many issues that may seriously impact the relationship with the client and it will vary from delivery to delivery. The first step is to accurately and honestly identify the driver/s of the issues being experienced in the current delivery, in the specific client relationship. Once those drivers are identified, develop, agree to, and implement action plans to resolve the issues. This effort is most effective as a collaborative effort with the appropriate Organization, and at the right time, client stakeholders.

Prevention Measures:

1. Identify Customer expectations and measurement for success as early as possible in, or preferably before, the project implementation. Determine Client's requirements for what meets minimum expectations. Set short range, one or two day, goals and report on progress daily to establish successes early in the project. Under-promise and over deliver where ever possible.

2. Escalate issues such as these as soon as possible to the Client's executive management team. Solicit Organization executive management support in these escalations as necessary.

3. The Project Executive is the key to the relationship. Communication with the Client must continue to take place with emphasis on the causes of the problems and resolution.

4. Contract with the Relationship Alignment Solutions group to address and improve the Client relationship.

5. Ensure use of strict Project Management discipline. In some cases more experienced PM resources may be required to manage the customer relationship.

6. Effectively utilize the Delivery Transition and kickoff meetings to identify and resolve mismatches in expectations.

7. Establish communication and collabor-

ation with the various Organization stake-holders in the account.

8. Ensure that the Customer's Conditions of Satisfaction are up-to-date, and validated with the client.

9. Review the project requirements with the customer. Identify and resolve any variances between the baseline and current solution SOW, and the customer's current requirements.

10. Establish and maintain frequent and clear communications with the customer. Utilize status reports and Change Management. Gain concurrence from the client on the most effective form(s) of on-going communication that will be used (phone, status meetings, status reports, face to face, email, etc...) and establish a protocol for how they will be used. For example, ensure that status meetings that are scheduled for 60 minutes do not go longer; ensure meetings have specific agendas (and stick to it); use time effectively (i.e. "net it out" if the client's availability is limited).

11. Validate that customer dependencies are included in the Project Schedule Plan and identify the schedule impact for tasks that are incomplete or delayed.

12. Strictly manage contract change.

13. Escalate to Organization management as appropriate.

5306. Client having financial problems

Description:
Economic conditions often cause Clients to have

financial difficulties, resulting in their inability to pay invoices promptly or in more serious situations the closure of a project. In these situations there is often little that Organization can do to prevent the problem, but there may be steps that can be taken to assist the Client through the financial problems.

Prevention Measures:

1. Involve Organization Credit Corporation to investigate financing for the project.
2. Investigate deferred billing arrangement.
3. Decrease scope to reduce cost.

5307. Ability to deliver project successfully is made difficult by the client's negative attitude toward Organization

Description:

In some situations the Client often becomes dissatisfied during the life of a project for one reason or another. One might argue that poor Client satisfaction is actually the result of other root causes occurring - and that is true. But in some situations the Client has become dissatisfied with Organization for some other reason and this can result in problems for the project manager and team. Ultimately the project manager has to work with his or her management and the Client to ensure that the Client is satisfied with the work on their project, regardless of the Client's other issues with Organization.

Prevention Measures:

1. Ensure the Client is advised of the Issues Management Process that should have been put in place at the beginning of the project and encouraged to use it to document the reasons for their dissatisfaction.

In other words, implement the Issues Management Process at the beginning of the project and ensure the Client is aware of the process and encouraged to use it.

2. During the implementation of any project, there will be some form of Client satisfaction issue. If the Organization PEs/PMs are doing there jobs effectively and in a disciplined fashion, this will be the case, especially in the areas of change control / scope management, adhering to the established entry and exit criteria, etc. A true measure of Client satisfaction is, did we deliver a quality solution on time, within the projected budget, that meets the Client's requirements.

3. Client dissatisfaction is usually the result of a long term problem, issue or misunderstanding. These causes cannot be fixed overnight. Consider bringing in an outside party, such as Relationship Alignment Solutions, to work with the Client and Organization to understand the root causes and develop solutions.

4. Conduct a Project Transition Meeting with the Proposal Team, Project Manager and Customer to assure all expectations, verbal and written, are clearly understood by the Customer and Delivery Team. Validate that the SOW meets the customer's requirements.

5. Use formal communications - Use written Status Reports to communicate accomplishments, schedules and open issues.

6. Communicate regularly with the customer

on an informal basis to foster ongoing communications and teamwork.

7. Consult with the customer, both users and management, and document their goals and priorities. Refer to this document regularly to ensure that Organization stays focused on the customer's goals and priorities. Ensure that a Customer Satisfaction Management plan is implemented and maintained throughout the project.

8. Establish strong Project Management disciplines for the team.

9. Ensure a Change Management process is strictly employed.

10. Document variances (and reasons thereof) and develop action plans to address the issues.

11. Notify Organization management of the issues.

5308. Inability to obtain, or limit security access to servers, or workstations

Description:
If Organization is assuming responsibility for running operations we must be able to control who has access to equipment such as servers and workstations. Without the appropriate access controls being in place we cannot ensure the security of the client's equipment and data. As roles and responsibilities are defined in the contract we must ensure that it clearly states that Organization will have the necessary access to servers and workstations.

Prevention Measures:

1. Specify access requirements in the contract.
2. Include any costs associated with obtaining or controlling access in the cost case.

5309. Inability to obtain customer documentation, or vendor documents

Description:

In order to fulfill our contractual responsibilities, Organization often needs access to customer or 3rd party documents which contain information about the systems and applications that we are taking responsibility for. Without this information Organization cannot perform its job. The customer has the responsibility to ensure that Organization gets the information it needs whether that documentation comes from their own personnel or from their 3rd party vendors.

Prevention Measures:

1. Ensure that in the contract's description of roles and responsibilities, the customer's responsibility to provide their own and 3rd party documentation is listed. The specific documents or types of documentation that are needed should be clearly defined.

Subcontractor Issues (5401 - 5403)

5401. Unfulfilled subcontractor responsibilities

Description:
Many of the Organization proposed solutions are

dependent on the performance of subcontractors. When Organization signs a contract with a Client, Organization is on the line to deliver regardless of whether the subcontractor can ultimately deliver.

Prevention Measures:

1. Thoroughly check references of the subcontractor for this type of solution.
2. Review the subcontractor's detailed project and staffing plans.
3. Require the subcontractor to provide detailed status reports and issue logs.
4. Monitor performance of the subcontractor closely
5. Allow for resources, money and the time in the project plan for Organization to review and, if necessary, correct the subcontractor's work product before delivery to the client.
6. Add schedule buffer to the Client contract to cover for delays and corrections in the subcontractor's work.
7. Develop a contingency plan for alternative resources and methods to back fill the subcontractor in case of default.
8. If Client requires Organization to use a particular subcontractor, then Organization should try to include a clause which allows Organization to terminate the contract if the subcontractor is unable or unwilling to complete its responsibilities.
9. Ensure the subcontractor's SOW is:
- consistent with the Organization Client SOW,

- detailed enough for Organization to assess the probability of success, and
- reviewed by Organization technical resources to assess viability.

10. Follow Organization procurement processes to engage subcontractor. Use nationally approved contractors where possible to apply leverage on poor performance.

11. If new subcontractor, or contractor required by Client, pay special attention to financial report provided by procurement.

12. Request references and follow up with previous Clients for level of satisfaction.

13. Ensure that the subcontractor project plans are detailed enough and the status reporting is frequent enough to provide the Organization project team with "Early Warning" of potential impacts to project schedules and costs, so that appropriate risk mitigation plans can be established and executed mitigate the exposures.

5402. Ineffective relationship between Organization and subcontractor

Description:

Situations may exist where the relationship between Organization and a subcontractor becomes ineffective. This usually occurs when the subcontractor tries to go around Organization and interact directly with the Client or when the subcontractor feels they are being treated unfairly by Organization from a financial perspective on the project. The breakdown of the Organization / subcontractor relationship can be devastating to the success of a project.

Prevention Measures:

1. Establish expectations on conduct and contractual obligations as soon as the subcontractor is engaged.
2. Advise the subcontractor of the legal issues involved in circumventing contracts.
3. Establish a win-win relationship with the subcontractor just as with the Client.
4. Ensure regular meetings are held with subcontractors to ensure issues are addressed and early warning on problems is obtained.
5. If possible, ensure alternate suppliers are available to perform the services. Organization resources may be an alternative is problem arise.
6. Enforce terms and conditions of the contract.

5403. Subcontractor cost overruns

Description:

It is often necessary to involve subcontractors on projects to supplement the Organization skills required to successfully deliver a project. It is mandatory that a Subcontractor SOW be agreed to and signed by both Organization and the subcontractor. This SOW should include estimates for providing the tasks and responsibilities assigned to the subcontractor and should be agreed to by both parties. There are instances, however, where these estimates are not accurate and results in overruns by the subcontractor.

Prevention Measures:

1. Ensure that a Subcontractor SOW is agreed to by both parties.

2. Ensure that the subcontractor was involved in developing the estimates and agrees to complete their tasks within the agreed-to estimates.

3. Include clauses in the Subcontractor SOW to hold the subcontractor responsible for their estimates and protect Organization from cost overruns.

4. During the engagement phase, thoroughly assess the capabilities and history of the subcontractors being considered. Identify their strengths and weaknesses and assess what level of assistance / support from Organization may be required to address those weak areas. These weak areas could be in project management, development, testing, etc. and will surely be highlighted during the execution of project. If not addressed they will be significant contributors to the cost overruns.

▼ Internal Organization Issues (5501 - 5511)

5501. Problems with OEM or Organization products

Description:
Several bids have been based on the assumption that an unannounced or new product would work in a new environment. However, it is sometimes the case that the products do not work as anticipated. In addition, certain Organization and OEM products are prone to problems if not properly used. Quick and adequate response from the product labs or

third party manufacturers is not always possible or forthcoming. A product need not be unannounced or new to cause unexpected problems in an integration project. There have been situations where products have been generally available for months, however, they did not integrate into a new environment as expected.

Prevention Measures:

1. Perform Organization product reviews as required by the WWQA Process.

2. Perform Organization Product Safety reviews as required by the WWQA Process.

3. Perform Technical and Delivery Assessment (TDA) reviews as required by the WWQA Process.

4. Conduct due diligence by modeling and testing the components to validate that they will work in the target environment.

5. The IGS Product Review Trigger Tool should be utilized to determine if the defined solution contains a product or products requiring an Organization Product Review. See Section 6 of the QA Information database for a link to the "trigger tool" and more information on the Product Review process.

6. Obtain a written commitment from the product lab or product owner outlining the level of support, cost and/or liability coverage you can expect to receive should problems arise with the product during the project.

7. Set appropriate Customer expectations. If

new or untested components are to be integrated as a part of the solution, the Client should understand that there will be risks of delays in the integration effort. If a Client wants 100% assurance of a fit, then a fully-tested solution of standard available products should be proposed.

8. If the Client wants leading (bleeding) edge components, then the Client should be made aware that a certain level of risk is inherent in implementing a solution in an untested environment. Conservative schedules and estimates should also be used to cover the unanticipated delays which invariably arise.

9. Conservative schedules and estimates should also be used to cover the unanticipated delays which invariably arise.

10. Be prepared to propose an alternate solution if the components do not integrate as expected.

11. Avoid the use of new products in an untested solution.

12. Increase the risk rating of the project and include appropriate cost and schedule allowances for risk response.

13. If the new system is to replace an existing system, do not plan on an immediate cutover. Plan for a pilot phase where both systems can run concurrently.

14. DOUs / Agreements should be drafted and agreed to by Organization and the respective OEM and Organization Product Labs / Support teams to provide timely support

in problem identification/resolution of any problems found related to their products.

5502. Technology / architecture issues

Description:

In some situations project teams may uncover bugs or problems with existing Organization technology and/or architectures that impact the success of their project. This is different than #5501 which involves relatively new products. This root cause involves products that are not new.

Prevention Measures:

1. Assuming that the SMEs conducting the Technical and Delivery Assessment (TDA) have the appropriate knowledge, experience and skills, these issues should be highlighted during the TDA reviews.

2. In the case of problems found in existing products, the Project Manager must ensure the appropriate process is followed for reporting the problem. When schedules are impacted, escalation must occur. On-site support from the product house should be requested to resolve the problem if normal methods have proved ineffective. On-site support should also be requested for key testing points on the schedule if additional problems are expected or critical situations are possible.

5503. Failure of Organization to fulfill responsibilities with Client or other Organization organization(s)

Description:

Under certain circumstances and situations Organization fails to fulfill responsibilities to a Client, mainly because one Organization has failed to fulfill its responsibilities to another Organization in delivering the contract. This generally occurs when one Organization is acting in the role of service provider whereby they do not own the contract and are working for recovery, not revenue. The other organization owns the contract, has direct responsibility for the delivery of the contract to the Client, and receives the revenue for the contract. Too often, the service provider resources are "pulled" to work on a revenue contract for their own organization without fulfilling their responsibilities on the other contract.

Prevention Measures:

1. Ensure a Document of Understanding (DOU) is agreed to between Organization organizations to clearly define expectations, time commitments, and expectations.

2. Secure executive sponsorship at the beginning of the project at a level that is sufficiently high to endorse any commitments.

3. The same expectations and criteria that we communicated to our subcontractors, must be applied to our Organization subs., with the same level of due diligence exercised.

4. Certainly there have been problems with this type of Organization interaction, the parties in revenue sharing projects can forget their focus and create parochial issues. The project lead must recognize this early and take steps to resolve the underlying

problem(s) before the Client is impacted.

5504. Organization project team morale or organizational issues

Description:

Team morale and organizational issues can often impact productivity and performance on a project. This is especially true when project resources are expected to work extraordinary amounts of overtime due to poor project estimating or lack of proper change management. This is especially true when they get no utilization credit and are not allowed to bill for their extra hours in order to keep project costs contained to the original estimate. Other factors such as unclear project definition and requirements can also impact the morale of the team.

Prevention Measures:

1. Ensure that all team members are aware of the project requirements and expectations.

2. Have project resources charge all time to the project - even though it may not be billed to the Client. This may impact gross profit, but team members will get utilization credit for the hours worked.

3. Execute the change management process for changes in scope so that team members aren't expected to deliver additional work for no additional hours.

4. Provide some team-building activities (dinners out, night at the movies, etc.). This only takes a little money - but can go a long way to keeping the resources on the project happy.

5505. Ineffective relationship between Organization organizations

Description:
With large complex projects it is often necessary to involve resources from more than one part of Organization. Performance targets and measurements are usually different and this often results in conflicts within the project team. Even worse, the Client frequently becomes aware of this internal conflict and then has the impression that Organization resources working on their project are not one team.

Prevention Measures:

1. Be sure that Documents of Understanding (DOUs) are written between the groups to validate expectations, roles & responsibilities, and commitments.

2. Conduct an Organization team meeting prior to work beginning at the Client to ensure that all parties understand the project organization, roles & responsibilities, tasks, deliverables, completion criteria, etc.

3. Secure executive sponsorship at the beginning of the project at a level that is sufficiently high to endorse any commitments.

4. When two or more Organization organizations are working together on a single project, ensure there is an integrated plan and a single interface to the Client.

5506. Organization / Third Party alliance issues

Description:
Some projects require the use of software, hardware,

or services personnel from third party suppliers with whom Organization has an alliance. These are typically our formal "business partners" and not simply subcontractors. There have been situations where associates from the third party alliances have bypassed Organization and tried to interact directly with the Client - even trying to convince the Client not to use Organization on the project. This causes a great deal of problems on the project and can impact Client satisfaction.

Prevention Measures:

1. Establish the project roles & responsibilities for the project very early - even before the contract has been signed, if possible.

2. Conduct a meeting with the third party alliance team members prior to meeting with the Client to establish the "game plan" for the project and get any issues resolved prior to starting work at the Client location.

3. Develop a well-defined communication and escalation plan.

4. Escalate any issues that surface immediately so that they can be resolved before the Client realizes there is a problem and the project becomes troubled.

5507. Multi-site development issues

Description:
For large, complex projects that require a large number of developers and/or delivery personnel, it may be necessary to involve resources from several

143

different locations. This makes the project much more difficult to manage because procedures and processes may vary by Organization location. Communication is often more complicated when multiple locations are utilized.

Prevention Measures:

1. Try to contain all work to a single Organization location.

2. If necessary to use multiple locations, try to assign groups of related tasks to each different Organization location.

3. Establish a clearly defined communication and issue escalation plan at the beginning of the project.

4. Subcontract Management disciplines and procedures apply.

5508. Global resourcing issues

Description:

In order to reduce the cost of delivering projects, Organization is implementing a global resourcing model. For situations where it is appropriate and beneficial, Organization may choose to use development resources that reside in a different geographical location than where the project is being delivered. Managing a project in these situations is often more complex because of time zone, language, or cultural differences.

Prevention Measures:

1. Establish a detailed communication and status reporting plan at the beginning of the project to ensure that the project manager and remote developers are kept in-

formed of work activities and issues.

2. Conduct regular status calls (not just written status reports) to validate current status.

3. Projects using global resources should have an interface person or project manager in the country contracting for the work. This will provide face time with the solution designers and end users to ensure the requirements are clearly understood. This person can then communicate to the global resources. They, in turn, will have a person who can answer questions or resolve issues who is familiar with their environment and the requesting party.

5509. Financial results negatively impacted by adjustments to internal cost allocations

Description:
A contract may be achieving its planned cost case and then be hit with unexpected cost allocations which have nothing to do with the contract but are applied by management to all contracts in the portfolio. As a result the contracts profitability is negatively impacted.

Prevention Measures:

1. Periodically review and adjust project financials with pricing to be prepared for new allocations not originally considered into the cost case.

2. Assess and document the total impact to the contract of all unexpected cost allocations.

3. If appropriate, request a financial rebase-lining of the contract. FROM FINANCE

4. Identify the negative variance as part of frequent variance analysis and manage through the Issues Management Plan

5510. Lack of technical leadership

Description:

Organization is responsible for providing the technical leadership required to ensure the proposed solution gets implemented correctly and meets the requirements. If we do not ensure that we have the resources in place to provide that leadership our ability to implement the solution is jeopardized

Prevention Measures:

1. Ensure that the Organization technical leaders have experience delivering the proposed solution.

2. If Organization has architectural control of the solution, ensure that an experienced architect is assigned to design, develop and deploy the solution.

3. If Organization just has responsibility for implementation of the solution (i.e. the client retains architectural control) ensure that the roles and responsibilities of both Organization and the client are clearly defined in the contract.

5511. Solution built does not match solution defined in contract

Description:

If the solution which is being delivered does not match what was defined in the contract Organization is at risk of not fulfilling its contractual obligations and dissatisfying the client. We must ensure that we are meeting the client's expectations about the solution to be provided. Any deviation must be discussed with the client and approved by them.

Prevention Measures:

1. Do not wait until deliverables are ready to find out if they will meet contract obligations. Schedule periodic quality assurance reviews through contract life.
2. Manage to all of the project baselines.
3. Implement strict Change and Quality Management discipline.
4. Don't perform any work without a signed SOW or PCA.

▼No Signed Contract (5601)

5601. Working without a signed contract or PCR/PCA

Description:

In many situations the Client is anxious to get their project started and asks Organization to begin work while still negotiating the SOW. In these situations Organization is often anxious to satisfy the Client's request and keep them happy. So the project team begins work without a signed SOW or contract. Beginning work without a signed SOW or contract exposes Organization to potential loss of revenue for work completed in the event that contract negotiations are not completed and a contract is not signed. There can also be insurance and security exposures for Organization associates working at a Client location without a signed contract. Working without a signed SOW or some other contractual document. **SHOULD NEVER BE DONE.**

Prevention Measures:

1. Prepare an Organization Letter of Authorization (LOA) that officially lets Organization start work on a project while the SOW or contract is still being negotiated. The LOA must be reviewed / approved by Quality Assurance prior to being given to the Client.

2. Ensure that no project team members are allowed to begin work until the SOW or LOA has been signed.

Reference QA Tip: Letter of Authorization, Organization Commitment Letter, Work@Risk, Early Start Letter, Letter of Intent

▼**Transition and Transformation (5701 - 5709)**

5701. Ineffective T&T project startup (SO)

Description:
As with any project, if T&T goes not get started in an organized and timely manner the probability of a successful completion will be jeopardized. As soon as services delivery begins, it is critical to have a detailed Transition plan in place so that transition activities can commence right away. Before Transition concludes a detailed Transformation plan should be developed so there can be a seamless progression from Transition to Transformation activities. Delays in adequately staffing the Transition will im-

pact the schedule and can cause delays in achieving planned milestones. Whether or not we are able to start T&T in an effective manner will leave a lasting impression with the client about our delivery capabilities.

Prevention Measures:

1. Make sure the Transition Manager is on board for the kickoff meeting with the customer.
2. Ensure the required resources identified in the staffing plan are on board to start T&T according to the schedule.
3. Ensure a Delivery Transition Review is conducted, results documented and an action plan put in place to resolve issues.

5702. Lack of or inadequate T&T project management plan/ schedule (SO)

Description:

A current project management plan/schedule is one of the fundamentals of good project management. Not having a current schedule for T&T results in the Transition manager being unaware of what tasks are due, what work has been completed, what work remains to be done, how many hours have been spent on a task, etc. Failure to maintain a project management schedule nearly always results in a troubled T&T project.

Prevention Measures:

1. Ensure that a current T&T project management plan/schedule was developed prior

to the start of the Transition and that it is kept current throughout the life of the T&T.

2. Ensure that the Transition Manager has the skills to create a project plan using a project planning tool such as Microsoft Project.

3. If needed, ensure that an experienced Project Administrator, preferably a Jr. PM, to assist the Transition Manager in the plan development, scheduling and tracking. Individuals in this role should have an in-depth knowledge in the use of whatever PM tool that will be used on the project.

4. Identify risks in the plan and develop mitigation actions. Build in an adequate amount of contingency in the plan with respect to risks that cannot be fully mitigated.

5703. Not properly using approved Organization methodology (GTTA) for T&T (SO)

Description:

Organization has spent a great deal of time and money developing various methodologies for project management and for technical delivery. These methodologies contain valuable information, work products, templates, etc. designed to help Transition teams improve efficiency and profitability on a project. Using these methodologies also creates a level of consistency between projects so that project team members are able to move between projects more easily. Not using one of the approved methodologies generally results in a "reinventing the wheel" and "starting from scratch" environment.

Prevention Measures:

1. Ensure that an approved Organization Transition management methodologies is being used on the project. GTTA (Global Transition and Transformation Architecture) is the approved methodology to be used for T&T (Transition and Transformation) and should be used for SO engagements.

2. Ensure that key members of the project team have the appropriate experience, skills and knowledge to effectively implement and execute the approved Organization methodology. Ensure that these resources are factored into the staffing plans and cost case during the engagement delivery phase.

5704. Ineffective T&T communications (SO)

Description:

It is critical that the T&T manager have an effective communications plan with the client, the project team, and Organization management. Troubled projects are often the result of simply not having regular status reporting, client meetings, project team meetings, etc. In these situations the client is unaware of the progress being made on a project. Without regular status reporting, the client is also unaware of issues that may need their involvement and attention. The same can be said for Organization management. Without proper and effective communications, everyone assumes that T&T is on schedule, on budget, and progressing as planned. Later, if T&T is in trouble, it is too late to start trying to document all of the issues that have contributed to the troubled status.

Prevention Measures:

1. Develop a communications / escalation plan at the beginning of T&T.

2. Ensure that regular communications and status reporting occur on a regular basis (as defined in the communications plan) with the client, project team, and Organization management throughout T&T.

5705. Ineffective T&T staffing (SO)

Description:
Our ability to execute the T&T ontime and within budget is very dependent on being able to staff the T&T from day one with the required number of resources who have the necessary skills to get the job done. Not effectively staffing the T&T in a timely manner jeopardizes our ability to have a successful T&T.

Prevention Measures:

1. Make sure an experienced Transition Manager is on board from day one.

2. Verify that the number of resources and their skill levels agree with what is in the staffing plan and the cost case.

3. If GR is being used to staff T&T ensure the schedule includes adequate time to get them on board and familiar with their

roles and responsibilities.

5706. Transition project closed without meeting all function, cost &/or schedule objectives

Description:
If the Transition project is closed before all the required activities are performed we create a false sense that the Transition project is 'complete'. There is still more work to be done and more costs to be incurred because the uncompleted objectives will still have to be met. Not correctly completing the Transition project will negatively impact client satisfaction and our ability to get to Transformation.

Prevention Measures:

1. Meet periodically with Transition Manager to understand the status of transition activities and, if required, adjust the end-to-end project plan accordingly.

5707. Transformation project closed without meeting all function, cost &/or schedule objectives

Description:
If the Transformation project is closed before all the required activities are performed we create a false sense that the Transformation project is 'complete'. There is still more work to be done and more costs to be incurred because the uncompleted objectives will still have to be met. Not correctly completing the Transformation project will negatively impact client satisfaction and our ability to get to Steady State.

Prevention Measures:

1. Meet periodically with Transformation Manager to understand the status of transformation activities and, if required, adjust the end-to-end project plan accordingly.

5708. Ineffective management of transition project

Description:

Just having a project plan in place doesn't ensure that a transition will be successful. A good Transition Manager must be in place to ensure that the required project management processes are being followed so the project plan can be executed successfully. If the Transition tasks are not carefully managed our ability to complete the Transition on time and on budget and meet the client's expectations will be jeopardized.

Prevention Measures:

1. Ensure an experienced Transition Manager is assigned to the engagement as early as possible during Solution Design.
2. Ensure there is a detailed transition plan in place.

5709. Ineffective management of transformation project

Description:

Just having a project plan in place doesn't ensure that a transformation will be successful. A good Transformation Manager must be in place to ensure that the required project management processes are being followed so the project plan can be executed successfully. If the Transformation tasks are not carefully managed our ability to complete the Transformation on time and on budget and meet the client's expectations will be jeopardized.

Prevention Measures:

1. Ensure an experienced Transformation Manager is assigned to the engagement as early as possible during Solution Design.
2. Ensure there is a detailed transformation plan in place prior to the end of Transition.

▼ Addenda Issues (SO) (5801 - 5808)

5801. Ineffective addenda project communications (SO)

Description:

It is critical that project managers have an effective communications plan with the client, the project team, and Organization management. Troubled projects are often the result of simply not having regular status reporting, client meetings, project team meetings, etc. In these situations the client is unaware of the progress being made on a project. Without regular status reporting, the client is also unaware of issues that may need their involvement and attention. The same can be said for Organization management. Without proper and effective communications, everyone assumes that the addenda project is on schedule, on budget, and progressing as planned. Later, if the project is in trouble, it is too late to start trying to document all of the issues that have contributed to the project's troubled status.

Prevention Measures:

1. Develop a communications / escalation plan at the beginning of the addenda project.
2. Ensure that regular communications and status reporting occur on a regular basis (as defined in the communications plan) with the client, project team, and Organization management throughout the life of the project.

5802. Ineffective addenda project startup (SO)

Description:
Failure of the Organization Project Manager and Client Project Manager to review the SOW as the appropriate definition of the addenda project scope. The Client should also be aware of the addenda project plan and if/how Client personnel will be used as a part of the overall project. See also #5102: Unclear / ineffective project organization.

Prevention Measures:

1. At the commencement of every addenda project, ensure that the Organization Project Manager reviews the SOW with the Client Project Manager and obtains full concurrence regarding the tasks, Organization and Client Responsibilities, deliverables, completion criteria, change control procedures, schedule, project organization and roles, etc.
2. If any disagreements occur, escalate as defined in the governance process to remedy the disagreement. Ensure that any result-

ing changes to the SOW are formally incorporated via the change control procedure before the project proceeds.

3. Hold a kickoff meeting to introduce team members and stakeholders to each other and to define roles and responsibilities. Use the kickoff meeting to:

- Define scope (not develop work breakdown)
- Identify the purpose of the project and expected output
- Identify potential risks and preliminary plans (hold additional risk management sessions throughout the project)
- Present immediate plans for the project and describe what each project team member will be doing in the next several days.

5803. Starting an addenda project phase prior to completing a preceding phase (SO)

Description:
Starting an addenda phase before a related preceding phase is complete is a risky decision. Much rework may be required as a result of work beginning prematurely. If the client has not agreed starting the next phase he may refuse to pay for the rework required. It has been proven time and time again that this tactic does not work.

Prevention Measures:

1. Ensure that the Project Manager plans and executes the addenda project in a manner that does not allow a phase (or task) to start before a dependent predecessor phase

has been completed.

2. Ensure that the Services Delivery Unit Management regularly assesses the status of the addenda project and is aware (by reading status reports and attending status meetings) of any decisions to start a phase before a prior phase has been completed.

3. For every addenda project Activity or Phase, entry and exit criteria must be documented, identifying the inputs, the outputs, and the validation process for determining if the entry / exit criteria have been met.

5804. Continuous/constant change in addenda project scope (SO)

Description:

Everyone understands that there will nearly always be changes in scope during the life of an addenda project. And there are usually change management processes in place to address these changes. But in some circumstances the Client makes continuous changes to the scope of an addenda project. Sometimes these requested changes are large and have a significant impact on the project. This usually occurs when the Client didn't have a clear understanding of what they wanted or frequently change their mind about what they want. While changes can be handled through change management, constant change in scope often means rework and frustration for the project team. It can also mean that the Project Manager is fully occupied with understanding, documenting and issuing change authorizations that they can't focus on the actual task of managing the addenda project.

Prevention Measures:

1. Ensure the scope and requirements are clearly identified and understood by all parties prior to starting work.
2. Be sure to incorporate the changes into the work breakdown structure and keep the Client constantly advised of the impact of the changes on the schedule as well as the cost. By doing so, the Client will understand the impact of the excessive changes on the schedule and price.
3. Schedule impacts, solution quality and stability impacts should be the main topics of discussion with the Client PM and Executives when trying to address this issue.
4. Ensure the contract Change Management process is enforced for all requested scope changes.
5. Include the impact / cost on the total addenda project for each change.
6. If changes are too frequent, try to establish a release plan. Create frequent releases which supply function to the Client to prevent the original plan from continuous extensions without deliverables.

5805. Lack of or inadequate addenda project management plan/schedule (SO)

Description:
A current project management plan/schedule is one

of the fundamentals of good project management. Not having a current schedule results in the project manager being unaware of what tasks are due, what work has been completed, what work remains to be done, how many hours have been spent on a task, etc. Failure to maintain a project management schedule nearly always results in a troubled project.

Prevention Measures:

1. Ensure that a current project management plan/schedule was developed prior to the start of the project and that it is kept current throughout the life of the project.

2. Ensure that the Project Manager has the skills to create a project plan using a project planning tool such as Microsoft Project.

3. Ensure that the project has assigned an experienced Project Administrator, preferably a Jr. PM, to assist the PM in the PM plan development, scheduling and tracking. Individuals in this role should have an indepth knowledge in the use of whatever PM tool that will be used on the project.

4. A contract which has multiple, related and/or dependent projects and phases requires an additional level of planning. An integrated plan for the entire group is required to ensure any dependencies are met. Client and subcontractor plans should be included. The integrated plan can be used to manage the project.

5806. Not properly using approved Organization project

management methodology for addenda projects (SO)

Description:

Organization has spent a great deal of time and money developing various methodologies for project management (WWPMM and PgMS) and for technical delivery (Unified Method Framework). These methodologies contain valuable information, work products, templates, etc. designed to help project teams improve efficiency and profitability on an addenda project. Using these methodologies also creates a level of consistency between projects so that project team members are able to move between projects more easily. Not using one of the approved methodologies generally results in a "reinventing the wheel" and "starting from scratch" environment.

Prevention Measures:

1. Ensure that one of the approved Organization project management methodologies (WWPMM or PgMS) is being used on the addenda project.

2. Ensure that Unified Method Framework is being used as the technical delivery methodology on the addenda project.

3. Ensure that key members of the project team have the appropriate experience, skills and knowledge to effectively implement and execute the approved Organization methodologies such as WWPMM and Unified Method Framework. Ensure that these resources are factored into the staffing plans and cost case during the engagement delivery phase.

5807. Ineffective addenda project staffing (SO)

Description:

It is important that staffing plans be accurate and complete. A well-defined staffing plan enables the Project Manager to know what skills will be needed on an addenda project and for how long. Without an effective staffing plan, the Project Manager is often unable to obtain the right skills at the right time.

Prevention Measures:

1. Ensure that a staffing plan is developed prior to the start of an addenda project.

2. Work with the appropriate Resource Deployment Managers (RDMs) or other staffing personnel to make them aware of what skills will be needed and when.

3. A project should always be staffed with resources that possess the appropriate skills, experience and knowledge to "jump start" the project and ensure successful delivery. Ineffective staffing plans are mainly a direct result of trying to staff the project with less expensive / lower band level resources in order to lower the cost.

4. Ensure a project plan is developed and used throughout the project life. This will ensure all tasks are staffed and any deficiencies are made visible at the earliest point in time.

5808. Ineffective management of addenda projects

Description:

Just having a project plan in place doesn't ensure that an addenda project will be successful. A good Project Manager must be in place to ensure that the required project management processes are being followed so the project plan can be executed successfully. If the tasks are not carefully managed our ability to complete the project on time and on budget and meet the client's expectations will be jeopardized.

Prevention Measures:

1. For each project identify a Project Manager who not only possess the proper skills, but also has had experience with the scope of the project and with the client's environment.

▼ Skills Availability Issues (5901 - 5911)

5901. Inability to acquired properly skilled resources which are not covered by the other root causes

Description:
If there is no root cause in the available list which identifies the skill set that cannot be acquired, then select this root cause. Make sure that the missing skill set is documented in the PMR report.

Prevention Measures:

1. N/A

5902. Inability to acquire RFS resources (SO)

Description:
Resources with the required skills cannot be obtained. They are either not available or cannot be

obtained at the band level planned in the cost case. When resources are not available to execute the RFS process it will result in delays. A backlog of RFS requests will cause client dissatisfaction and reduce the amount of addenda revenue that can be generated.

Prevention Measures:

1. When reviewing the staffing plan ensure that adequate resources are included to address the anticipated volume of RFS activity.

2. Prior to contract signing, validate that the required resources, with the necessary skills, will be available when needed to implement and execute the RFS process.

5903. Inability to acquire Program/Project Management Office resources (SO) (Global business services)

Description:

Resources with the required skills cannot be obtained. They are either not available or cannot be obtained at the band level planned in the cost case. The Program / Project must be adequately staffed so that the PMPs needed to effectively manage the contract can be implemented and executed.

Prevention Measures:

1. Prior to contract signing, validate that the required resources, with the necessary skills, will be available when needed Validate that the required resources, with the necessary skills, will be available when

needed.

5904. Inability to acquire Delivery resources (SO)

Description:
Resources with the required skills cannot be obtained. They are either not available or cannot be obtained at the band level planned in the cost case. If the necessary Delivery resources are not available when needed we will not be able to meet our contractual commitments. Missing scheduled milestones, deliverables or SLAs can result in penalties and impact both client satisfaction and contract profit.

Prevention Measures:

1. When reviewing the staffing plan ensure that adequate resources are included to meet the delivery schedule.
2. Prior to contract signing, validate that the required resources, with the necessary skills, will be available when needed.

5905. Inability to acquire T&T resources (SO)

Description:
Our ability to execute the T&T ontime and within budget is very dependent on being able to staff the T&T with the required number of resources who have the necessary skills to get the job done. Resources with the required skills cannot be obtained. They are either not available or cannot be obtained at the band level planned in the cost case.

Prevention Measures:

> 1. Prior to contract signing, validate that the required resources, with the necessary skills, will be available when needed.

5906. Inability to acquire SAP resources (Global business services)

Description:
Resources with the required skills cannot be obtained. They are either not available or cannot be obtained at the band level planned in the cost case.

Prevention Measures:

> 1. Prior to contract signing, validate that the required resources, with the necessary skills, will be available when needed.

5907. Inability to acquire PM resources (Global business services)

Description:
Resources with the required skills cannot be obtained. They are either not available or cannot be obtained at the band level planned in the cost case.

Prevention Measures:

> 1. Prior to contract signing, validate that the required resources, with the necessary skills, will be available when needed.

5908. Inability to acquire Architect resources (SO) (Global business services)

Description:
Resources with the required skills cannot be obtained. They are either not available or cannot be obtained at the band level planned in the cost case.

Prevention Measures:

1. Prior to contract signing, validate that the required resources, with the necessary skills, will be available when needed.

5909. Inability to acquire Application Development resources (Global business services)

Description:
Resources with the required skills cannot be obtained. They are either not available or cannot be obtained at the band level planned in the cost case.

Prevention Measures:

1. Prior to contract signing, validate that the required resources, with the necessary skills, will be available when needed.

5910. Inability to acquire SOA resources (Global business services)

Description:
Resources with the required skills cannot be obtained. They are either not available or cannot be obtained at the band level planned in the cost case.

Prevention Measures:

1. Prior to contract signing, validate that the required resources, with the necessary

skills, will be available when needed.

5911. Inability to acquire GDC-AD resources (Global business services)

Description:

Resources with the required skills cannot be obtained. They are either not available or cannot be obtained at the band level planned in the cost case.

Prevention Measures:

1. Prior to contract signing, validate that the required resources, with the necessary skills, will be available when needed.

NOTES

NOTES

NOTES

NOTES

2 CHAPTER 2 – GOLDEN RULES FOR PROJECTS SUCCESS

2.1.　　APPROACH

> ➤ Set-up the Project
> ➤ Understand the Requirements
> ➤ Create the Team
> ➤ Construct the Plan
> ➤ Execute the Plan
> ➤ Sign-off on Project upon its completion
> ➤ Recognize the team and celebrate success

A project checklist is a useful artifact to include in the project.
"Good checklists, on the other hand, are precise. They are efficient, to the point, and easy to use even in the most difficult situations. Good checklists are, above all, practical."

Depending on which study you want to believe, the success rate for projects is between 30% and 70%. The Standish Group researches and produces reports on IT projects' success rates as measured upon original estimates of scope, schedule, and budget. The 2013 report found that only 39% of IT projects achieved an on-scope, on-schedule, and on-budget delivery, with 43% of projects identified as "challenged" (over budget or late), and 18% cancelled or never implemented. An-other IT project success rate study, this one performed by Dr. Dobb's Journal in 2010, asked participants to rate success based on the identified success criteria of their projects rather than by the "on-schedule and on-budget" definition. The

Dr. Dobb's numbers are a little more encouraging than The Standish Group's but probably lower than most project managers and their sponsors would consider acceptable:

- Ad-hoc projects: 49% are successful, 37% are challenged, and 14% are failures

- Iterative projects: 61% are successful, 28% are challenged, and 11% are failures

- Agile projects: 60% are successful, 28% are challenged, and 12% are failures

- Traditional projects: 47% are successful, 36% are challenged, and 17% are failures.

2.2. CRITICAL SUCCESS FACTORS FOR IT PROJECTS SUCCESS

• End to end End-User involvement from 1st day till closure of the Project - Engaged and active executive sponsors are paramount to project success.

• Continuous Executive Management support

• Clear Business objectives, use of checklists and Quality Gates approach

• Experienced Project Managers

• Minimized Scope and Requirements / prevention of scope creep, clear Project vision

• Being agile way of working and use of relevant DevOps tools and adopting relevant XP practices

• Skilled Resources, self-motivated cross functional teams

• Formal Methodology, use of continuous pro-active risks & issues management

• Good financial Management

• Use of Standard Tools & Infrastructure, best practices & lessons learnt and reuse of assets, accelerators

• Have team retrospectives, continually improve based on customers & competitors feedback.

• Submit monthly Metrics and weekly PM 7 Keys on time. Track costs, effort hours, rework and project errors.

• Meticulous updating of the project work plan to ensure it is up-to-date and that it always shows a clear path to completion.

• Measure client satisfaction with the recovery. This includes sending out short client satisfaction surveys, as well as talking first-hand with the major stakeholders to ensure that their expectations are being met, capturing product/ process CSAT score from customers at specified frequency..

• Define exit criteria for each client deliverables, create RACI for all stakeholders

• Sustain

Catching your Projects before they're troubled.

Examine the four types of classic mistakes:

    a. People-related

    b. Process-related

c. Product-related

d. Technology-related.

Establish a continuous improvement system by ensuring all deliverables and completion criteria are clearly defined, and that you have a separate quality assurance function to verify the deliverable. Integrate the above items into a process-related, closed-loop process to drive changes and prevent recurrences.

Assessing and working to recover troubled projects can be among the most difficult work a project manager ever has to perform. However, the payoff—whether for an RPM or the actual project manager—is huge. You've saved a project from failure status and have provided significant value to the organization. The five steps outlined in this paper are crucial for monitoring your projects and improving them before they reach "failed" status. Some key tips for each of the five steps include:

a. Do not declare victory too soon

b. Sustained control is necessary

c. Involve all stakeholders—politics are key

d. At the first sign of trouble, define the problem and solution and alert the stakeholders.

Sometimes a little extra effort in inspection, analysis and planning can make the difference between a failed project and a successful one. You just need to know the right way to do it.

If the project does not already have these in place, they need to be added as a part of the recovery plan. If they are already in place, the effectiveness of the processes needs to be validated, and other proactive activities may need to be added as well. Remember that the old processes for monitoring and measuring the work may not have been effective and may have contributed to the project getting into trouble. Stronger monitoring and measuring may be needed as a part of the recovery.

Depending on the duration remaining on the project, this may also be a time when the project manager needs to use techniques for micromanagement. Normally, you might not want to be involved in the team work activities on a detailed basis. However, when you are in a recovery, you may need to keep a close watch and close follow-up on all outstanding work.

In order to identify what to measure, a Project Management Organization should do the following:

    a. Identify what's important to project success

    b. Identify project manager behaviours that lead to success

    c. Align those behaviours to measurable goals

    d. Measure and report.

Success is never final, failure is never fatal. It's courage that counts.

—John Wooden

• Clear business objectives are crucial to project success because they set the direction for the team, should be the basis for most project decisions, and provide a clear and measureable criteria for declaring a project complete.

• Business objectives should follow the structure of SMART goals to ensure clear understanding and measurability.

• Without clear business objectives, you run the risk of delivering a product or solution that does not meet expectations or cannot be declared complete.

2.3. WHY IT IS CRITICAL

a. Doing more with less: Using the standard PMI etc. processes of Project management delivering projects on time, on budget with good FIRST TIME RIGHT product quality in an iterative and incremental way to deliver shippable products based on customer priority

b. Faster time to market by adopting Agile

c. Less risk factor

d. More ROI

e. Starting with best practices (SAP Activate methodology, Agile SCRUM, KANBAN, DevOps)

f. Customer delight, customer retention enabling base account growth.

A project management council is a silver bullet to bridge the gap between executives and project managers to achieve project successes. Effective use of Project Management principles and best practices make us work faster, better, cheaper.

A good Project Manager can make changes on the fly and adjust & adapt to enterprise needs.

The widespread use of metrics and measurements will guarantee success. Use crashing, fast tracking etc. technique (as and when required) to get things done faster.

2.4. GENERIC CAUSES OF PROJECTS FAILURE

➢ Expectations that are too high, unrealistic, not managed, or poorly communicated
➢ Requirements that are unclear, contradictory, ambiguous, or imprecise; or there is a lack of agreement on these requirements
➢ A lack of resources, resource conflicts, turn-over of key resources, or poor resource planning
➢ Planning that is based on insufficient data, missing items, insufficient details, or poor estimates.

2.5. FIRST THINGS FIRST - IS THE PROJECT REALLY IN TROUBLE?

When you are looking at a "troubled" project, the first thing to validate is whether the project is, in fact, in trouble or not. In many cases there is the perception of a problem when there really is not one at all. In other cases, a project may be in trouble, but the project manager might already have begun a process of damage control and correction. Sometimes the project has problems, but the problems are not significant enough for the project to be considered troubled. For instance, if a nine-month project is scheduled to complete a week late, you would need to decide whether it really is in trouble.

So, first validate that you actually have a problem by seeing whether the project is within acceptable tolerances. For more information on tolerances, see 40.1 Project Tolerances.

It is important to understand your tolerances because the project may be trending over budget or past the deadline, but it still may be in an acceptable ranges and not considered a troubled project.

2.6. CAN THE PROJECT BE TURNED AROUND QUICKLY?

If the project is in trouble, but not yet a disaster, see if you can determine the cause of the problem as well as put in place a quick turnaround plan. The project manager may already have a recovery plan in place or may need some help. However, the implication at this point is that the damage is minor and that the project can get back on track with a little more attention and a proactive plan. Sometimes this is referred to as a "soft" rescue. In many cases a soft rescue can turn the project around without any incremental impact in budget or schedule. That is, the activities associated with the rescue will be related to things like implementing better project management processes or swapping similar resources. If the project is too far gone for these types of relatively minor changes, more radical intervention will be required.

Some common project problems and potential solutions are described below.

- Problem #1 - Inadequate Project Definition and Planning
- Problem #2 - Poor Scope Management
- Problem #3 - Not Managing the Work plan
- Problem #4 - Poor Communication

• Problem #5 - Poor Quality Management

2.7. DEFINING A TROUBLED PROJECT

A troubled project can be defined as a project that exhibits at least one of the following criteria (plus or minus acceptable variances):

➤ Project exceeds the estimated budget
➤ Project is behind the estimated schedule
➤ Project is not meeting expected requirements
➤ Project's overall quality is unacceptable.

Defining the attributes of a troubled project is the first step in establishing a process for assessing and recovering projects. Organizations must then establish a set of evaluation criteria to assist in screening projects for potential review and recovery activities. These screening criteria should comprise a balanced set of measures for evaluating and identifying troubled projects, including financial, staffing, schedule, technical and business alignment measures. Using a set of established criteria in a standardized approach to evaluating projects helps to make the categorization of troubled projects an objective activity. The use of these criteria may also be incorporated into the organization's project portfolio review and reporting processes.

At this point, you have validated that the project is probably in trouble. You verified that the project is outside of any defined tolerances that have been defined for your organization. You also have done a quick check to determine that there is not a simple cause and remedy that can be put into place quickly. You should be able to put some criteria in place for what a troubled project looks like. The following criteria provide some examples:

 • The project is trending 30% or more over its estimated budget

 • The project is trending 30% or more over its estimated deadline (although this may not be as important if the budget is not also over by 30% or more).

 • The project appears within tolerances, but only by deferring the completion of one or more major deliverables.

 • The project appears within tolerances, but only by compromising on quality to the point that the value and integrity of the deliverable are called into question.

 • The client is extremely dissatisfied with the performance of the project team. If the client had to do it again, he or she would not use the same project team.

 • The client - project team relationship is dysfunctional. This could include situations such as the client and sponsor losing interest in the success of the project, major animosity between the project team and the client, deliberate sabotage by one party to make the other party look bad, etc.

All projects should be funded based on delivering some business value. However, as the project progresses, the business justification gets weaker. When this happens, the project should be canceled. However, this is not an example of a troubled project, per se. That is, there is not necessarily a problem with the project itself, and there is nothing that needs to be rescued. The project may then be canceled based on a normal business evaluation and not because of its troubled project.

Similarly, the business case for the project may have been unsound to begin with. The project could end successfully, but the business value gained may not live up to expectations. Again, a project in this situation would not be classified as troubled.

2.8.
CHARACTERISTICS OF A TROUBLED PROJECT

➢ No one has a firm idea of when the project will be finished and most people have given up trying to guess

➢ The product is laden with defects

➢ Team members are working excessive hours—20 or more hours per week of involuntary overtime

➢ Management has lost its ability to control progress or even to ascertain the project's status with any accuracy

➢ The customer has lost confidence that the project team will ever deliver the promised goods

➢ The team is defensive about its progress

➢ Relations between project team members are strained

- ➤ The project is on the verge of cancellation

- ➤ The morale of the project team has hit rock bottom

- ➤ The customer is threatening legal action

2.9.   ESSENTIAL CRITERIA FOR DETECTING TROUBLED PROJECTS

Financial Risk – the project is expected to exceed the budget at completion by more than 10%.

Scope Change – the number of approved scope changes exceeds a given threshold

Work Effort – the number of actual hours is exceeding budgeted hours by a significant percentage.

Schedule Milestones – there are significant gaps (greater than 5% over plan) between planned and actual milestone dates or completed deliverables; or no established milestone dates.

Quality Issues – the number of defects, errors, or review issues are critical and/or significantly growing during the project lifecycle.

Customer Relationship – the project team has a poor working relationship with the customer and/or the working relationship is rapidly declining.

2.10. PROJECT RECOVERY PROCESS

Turning around a troubled project is never easy, but there are approaches that can be used that will give you a good chance at success. (Remember that success does not mean reaching the original expectations and commitments. It is probably too late for that.) The assumption now is that we have a substantial project that is in trouble. It is out of acceptable tolerances and a remedy cannot be implemented easily and simply. For these troubled projects, the remedy is more than just "fix it." The following project turnaround model can be used:

- Define and Plan Recovery Project
- Assess the Troubled Project
- Develop a Recovery Plan
- Activate the Recovery Plan
- Measure and Monitor the Recovery Plan.

2.11. THE PURPOSE OF RECOVERY

Recovery is defined as saving a project from loss and restoring it to usefulness. The recovery approach outlined in this paper will focus on meeting the business case objectives as either established at the outset of the project or revised as a result of the assessment phase, which is the most likely scenario. The ART's main goals in recovery are:

➢ Producing an achievable schedule
➢ Re-establishing customer and management confidence
➢ Re-baselining the project plan
➢ Sorting project problems
➢ Rebuilding the original project team.

When faced with recovering a troubled project, there are three fundamental approaches:

➢   Reduce the project's scope, which speeds time to completion
➢   Increase productivity by focusing on short-term improvements
➢ Slip the schedule to satisfy the scope objectives.

2.12.   MANAGING THE RECOVERY PROCESS: THE ROLE OF THE PMO

An organization's Project Management Office (PMO) or enterprise-wide Strategic Project Office (SPO) typically functions in a number of important ways to improve and standardize project management practices across the organization. The function, governance structure, and span of control can vary by organization, but typical PMO and SPO functions include:

1. Project Controls
2. Processes, Standards, and Methodologies
3. PM Tools
4. Training
5. Direct Management of Projects
6. Consulting and Mentoring
7. Project Review and Recovery

A project review and recovery process should be a part of the PMO's functions to apply a consistent approach to evaluating projects whose outcomes have impact on the organization as a whole. Implementing a project review and recovery process that is administered by the PMO can help organizations recover the projects by applying sound project management practices in a focused and coherent manner. According to 2007 CBP research on The State of the PMO, this role is common among mature enterprise-level PMOs.

2.13. CRITICAL SUCCESS FACTORS FOR PROJECT RECOVERY

Project and recovery teams need to manage a number of critical factors to ensure a successful project recovery.

These factors include:

> Cultivating and controlling communication with all project stakeholders to manage expectations, encouraging honest and frank information exchange, and sharing knowledge gained in the process

> Using project managers experienced in turning around projects, or recovery specialists, to lead the Project Review and Recovery process

> Identifying projects in need of recovery as early as possible in their project lifecycle

> Establishing a sense of urgency and a heightened level of control in managing requirements, schedule, costs, risks, and changes to the original scope

> Monitoring stakeholder satisfaction throughout the recovery process

> Prioritizing non-essential objectives and requirements and conducting tradeoff analyses to deliver the best solution.

2.14. CLAIMING PROJECT RECOVERY SUCCESS

How do you determine if the project review and/or recovery were successful? How do you decide if the review and recovery processes brought value to your organization?

The simple answer may be "we know we are successful when the project delivered meets customer expectations while minimizing variances in schedule or cost." However, the more tangible factors indicating a successful review and recovery may include:

➢   Demonstrated cost savings or avoided opportunity cost; when a repository of data about similar projects exists, these metrics provide the strongest benefit case
➢   Stakeholders sharing a common vision of the project, including the project status, and the objectives/requirements that are being delivered
➢   Resolution of most or all project issues
➢   Development of an achievable schedule agreed upon by all stakeholders
➢   The end of negotiating and updating project baselines
➢   Stakeholders confident in the project team and overall project performance.

2.15.   PROJECT TOLERANCES

You have all read the stories about the large number of projects that fail. Depending on the report you read, half or more of all projects fail - perhaps as many as 80%! According to the reports, the larger the project, the greater the chance is that it will be a failure. However, as you look at the projects in your company, would you really say that 80% of them are failures? Would even 50% be considered failures? There is no doubt that some projects are absolute failures. They either crash and burn, and are canceled, or they finish dramatically over budget, over deadline, and under expectations. However, are there really 50%-80% that meet this definition?

2.16.
TOLERANCES

Tolerances

To answer the question of how many failed projects there are, you first need to understand the definition of a failed project. The concept that plays a key role is the idea of tolerances. If you estimate that a project will cost $230,000, is your project a failure if the actual cost is $230,500? You missed your budget, right? Yes, but this gets into the concept of tolerances. If you delivered within $500 on a $230,000 budget, you should be lifted on the group's shoulders and paraded around the company as a hero.

Your company needs to establish the tolerance level that it considers to be reasonable for projects. At some companies, for instance, the tolerance level is set at -10% to +5%. That is, if you delivered the project for 5% over budget, it was still considered a success. For our $230,000 project, this means we could have gone over budget by $11,500 and still been considered successful.

On the other side, if the final cost was under budget by more than 10%, that would also have been a problem. In this case, the problem is that the company wants to deliver projects within expectations. If the sponsor had known that the project actually costs a lot less than estimated, they may have been able to make other decisions with the unused budget. The cost estimate should also include any formally approved scope changes. If your original budget was $200,000, and the client approved an additional $30,000 in scope changes, then the final $230,000 is the number that you get held accountable for, plus your tolerances.

Normally there is room for tolerances with your deadline as well. If you estimate a project at six months, and it is completed in six months and one week, that is normally acceptable. Your original deadline must also be extended if scope changes have been approved. Of course, not all projects have that flexibility. The YR2K software projects, for instance, typically had to be completed by December 31, 1999. A week late was not going to work.

2.17. DECLARING SUCCESS FROM A PROJECT PERSPECTIVE

Once you understand what your tolerances are (if any), you can start to evaluate the success of the project. Generally, the project team members can declare success if:

1. The project is delivered within the estimated cost, plus or minus the tolerance.

2. The project was delivered within its deadline, plus or minus the tolerance.

3. All of the major deliverables were completed. (Some minor ones, or minor functionalities, might not be delivered.)

4. The overall quality is acceptable. (It does not have to be perfect.)

Some companies also look at whether the project team was easy to do business with. That is, did the client and the project team work well together? For instance, was there good communication? If the client had another project (and a choice), would they ask you to work on it again?

2.18. DECLARING SUCCESS FROM AN ORGANIZATION PERSPECTIVE

Declaring success from a project perspective is normally what the project team is asked to be accountable for. However, from a company perspective, success is also based on whether the company received the value that was promised from the initial ROI calculations. If the project was a failure from a "project" perspective, it is normally a failure from a company perspective as well. (Although this is not always the case; some projects are delivered way over their budget and deadline, yet the solution is still considered an overall business success.) However, there are also many examples of projects that were successfully delivered, yet are not delivering the value promised. If the project team delivered successfully within tolerances, there is usually nothing else that can be done from their perspective. However, it is possible that the return on investment (ROI) calculations were faulty, or the marketplace was misjudged by the client and the sponsor. It is also possible that this project was part of a larger initiative. Although your project may be successful, the overall, larger initiative may be a failure.

Every organization should have some general rules about how to declare the overall project a success or failure. Your project isn't a failure if you miss the budget by a dollar and deliver a day late. Normally, a project will still be considered successful if it delivers within cost and deadline tolerances, and delivers all major deliverables with an acceptable quality. However, from an overall business perspective, another set of questions should also be answered as to whether the business value was achieved as promised.

2.19.   POSSIBLE DECISIONS BASED ON THE PROJECT REVIEW

➢ Let the project continue (as-is)
➢ Cancel the project
➢ Direct the project manager and team to implement improvement recommendations
➢ Revise delivery dates
➢ Revise budgets
➢ Reduce scope
➢ Add more resources to accomplish more work
➢ Add or change resources to bring in new skills
➢ Increase the level of work through overtime

2.20.   PROJECTS GENERIC PROBLEM AREAS AND CONTINGENCY PLANS

Project Problem #1 - Inadequate Project Definition and Planning

Have you ever attended an end-of-project meeting on a project that had major problems? If you have, chances are that one of the major themes you will hear is that "we should have spent more time planning." Many project managers think that they need to jump right into the project by gathering business requirements. They think that if they do a good job gathering the business requirements, they are ready to run on the project. That is not true. In fact there is a definition and planning process that needs to happen before you ever start gathering the business requirements.

Before the project work begins, the project manager must make sure that the work is properly understood and agreed to by the project sponsor and key stakeholders. The project manager works with the sponsor and stakeholders to ensure that there is a common perception of what the project will deliver, when it will be completed, what it will cost, who will do the work, how the work will be done, and what the benefits will be. The larger the project, the more important it is that this information be mapped out formally and explicitly. All projects should start with this type of upfront planning to prevent future problems caused by differing viewpoints on the basic terms of the project.

Common Planning Problems

If you have poor up-front definition and planning, it will cause problems in many areas later in the project. These problems include:

• **Lack of business support:** If you do not define the major characteristics of a project up-front, it is very common to have differences in expectations among the major stakeholders. This is true even if you take all of your initial direction from the sponsor. As a project gets larger, even the sponsor may not have a totally complete picture of what needs to happen for the project to be successful. Other times, the sponsor has a vision, but there are other visions that may be better or more viable. These competing ideas end up surfacing later in the project and causing confusion and rework.

• **Poor estimates:** Usually a project needs to have a budget and deadline before the business requirements are completed. In many cases, if the definition and planning is not done ahead of time, the project team starts off with inadequate resources and time, and you don't realize it until the project is already in progress. Many projects that could be successful are viewed as failures because they overshot their budget and deadline. This situation is often caused by the project manager committing to numbers that are too low, the result of a lack of up-front planning.

• **Poor scope control:** One of the major aspects of defining a project is defining the high-level scope. If you do not define and gain agreement on scope, you will find it very difficult to manage scope effectively throughout the project.

How to Avoid the Mistake

Spending time on a good definition and planning ends up taking much less time and effort than having to correct problems while the project is underway. It should not be surprising, then, that the best way to avoid this problem is to do a good job of defining and planning the project up-front. This includes:

• **Defining:** Before the actual work of the project begins, make sure you have spent the time to define the project objectives, scope, assumptions, risks, budget, timeline, organization and overall approach. The project manager may think that they know all of this already. However, the purpose of this work is to ensure that there is a consensus between the project manager, project sponsor and all other stakeholders. Even if the project manager and the sponsor are in agreement, there may be other major stakeholders that have other ideas. Differences of opinion need between the major stakeholders needs to be resolved before the project starts – not while you are in the middle.

• **Planning:** The project manager should create an overall project work plan before the project starts. This will help you estimate the total project effort and duration. The project manager also needs to ensure that he or she has the detailed work mapped out over the next few months to ensure that the project resources are assigned the right work once the project actually begins.

In addition, it is very helpful to have an agreed upon set of Project Management Procedures that are used to manage the project. These will include how the project manager will manage scope, issues, risks, communication, the work plan, etc. Again, the key is to define these all up-front to better manage expectations. For instance, if you define and get agreement on the procedure for approving scope change requests, you should have a much easier time managing change once the project begins.

Project Problem #2 - Poor Scope Management

In the SoW/Contract please define properly approved baselines scope including functional and NFRs alongwith risks, assumptions etc. In Agile SCRUM we are giving delivery of shippable product features in incremental and iterative way based on customer priority, and it in turns prevents unnecessary scope creep.

• The types of deliverables that are in scope and out of scope. (Business Requirements, Current State Assessment)

• The major life-cycle processes that are in scope and out of scope. (Analysis, design, testing)

• The types of data that are in scope and out of scope. (Financial, sales, employee)

• The data sources (or databases) that are in scope and out of scope. (Billing, General Ledger, Payroll)

• The organizations that are in scope and out of scope. (Human Resources, Manufacturing, vendors)

• The major functionality that is in scope and out of scope. (Decision support, data entry, management reporting)

Have a Viable Scope Change Process in Place

The project manager and project team must realize that there is nothing wrong with scope change. That is, changing scope while a project is underway is not an evil proposition. In fact, in many cases it is a good thing. First, the client typically cannot identify every requirement and feature that will be required for the final solution. Second, even if they did, the business changes over time, and therefore the requirements of the project may change as well.

If you cannot accommodate change, the final solution may be less valuable than it should be, or it may, in fact, be unusable. Therefore, you want the client to have the ability to make changes during the project when needed. The problem comes when the project manager does not proactively manage change on the project. Every project should have a process in place to manage change effectively. The process should include identifying the change, determining the business value of the change, determining the impact on the project and then taking the resulting information to the project sponsor for his/her evaluation. The sponsor can determine if the change should be included. If it is included, the sponsor should also understand the impact on the project and allocate the additional budget and time needed to include the change.

Common Problems with Scope Change Management

There are a number of common problems that project teams encounter with scope change management.

• Scope creep: Many project managers recognize large scope changes, but are not as diligent about smaller changes. There is a tendency to just go ahead and add the additional work without too much thought. Scope creep refers to what happens when a project accepts a large number of small changes. When all of these small changes are combined, the team realizes that they have taken on too much extra work and can no longer meet their budget and deadline commitments.

• No sponsor approval: Many times a project manager will receive requests for changes from end users, stakeholders or client managers. Since these are all people in the client organization, there is a tendency to think that they should be accepted. Again, this is a mistake. The end users usually surface scope change requests, but they cannot approve them. Even a client manager cannot approve scope change requests. The only person that can is the sponsor (unless the sponsor has delegated this authority to others). Many projects get in trouble because the team thinks they are getting approval to proceed with scope changes, but discover later that the person that really counts, the sponsor, has not agreed.

• Project team accountability: Since the project team members can have a lot of interaction with the client, they are the ones that field scope change requests the most often. Therefore, the entire project team must understand the importance of scope change management. All of them must detect scope changes when they occur and funnel them back to the project manager. If they take on the extra work themselves, there is a good likelihood their activities will be completed late and jeopardize the entire project.

It's Never Too Late to Start

If you find that your project is starting to trend over its budget and schedule, try to find the cause. In many cases, you will find that you are simply taking on more work than you originally agreed to. The best time to define a scope change management process is before the project begins (as a part of the Project Management Procedures). However, if you do not have a good process in place, it is never too late to start. The project manager must call a quick time-out and work with the client on a process for detecting and approving scope change requests. Then, everyone must be educated in the new process. If there is a good side of this effort, it is that the team and the client can see firsthand the impact of not controlling scope because the project is already in trouble. They should be better able to understand the purpose of scope change management and be more willing to follow the more rigorous process in the future.

Project Problem #3 - Not Managing the Work plan

During the first part of the project, the project manager must spend the time required to define and plan the project. The result of defining a project is the completion of a Project Definition (also called a Project Charter and / or Project Scope Statement). The result of planning the project is the project work plan. The work plan is a vital tool to ensure that the project manager and project team know what they need to do to complete the project. Different approaches should be taken in this step according to the size of the project. The work plan for small projects can be built without a lot of formality. Larger projects usually require a work plan built by using a previous work plan from a similar project or by building a work plan from scratch using the Work Breakdown Structure (WBS) technique. The WBS is a technique for looking at the project at a high level, and then subsequently breaking the work into smaller and smaller pieces until you can get the full picture of the totality of work that needs to be performed.

The Warning Signs

Many project managers think that the creation of the original project work plan is the end of the effort. There are a couple signs that the work plan is not being updated.

• The project manager cannot tell you exactly what work is remaining to complete the project.

• The project manager is unsure whether the project will be complete on-time and within budget.

• The project manager does not know the critical path of activities.

• Team members are not sure of what work they need to start next (or even what they should be working on now).

The general sign that a project is in trouble is that the project manager has a work plan, but does not really understand the progress made to date and how much work is remaining. When this happens, the project team is not utilized efficiently on the most critical activities. Ultimately, the project team gets toward the end of the project and realizes that they have much more work on their plate that anticipated, since earlier scheduled work is not yet completed. The team may also discover that they have rework to do, since earlier required steps were not completed.

Other Common Mistakes When Managing the Work plan

The biggest mistake project managers make is that they do not update the work plan at all once the project completes. However, there are a number of other common problems that occur.

• Infrequent updates: Sometimes the project manager updates the work plan, but at lengthy intervals - for instance, every two months on a six month project. The problem is that by the time you make a formal update, you may have already missed some activities. In addition, if you are behind schedule or over budget, it takes too long to notice, and you may be too far behind to make up the difference.

• Managing by % completion rather than completed fully on-time and tracking the schedule variance (actual vs. planned).

Project Problem #4 Poor Project Communication

• People are impacted by the project at the last minute. This is a prime cause of problems. In this situation, the project manager does not communicate proactively with other people about things that will impact them. When the communication does occur, it is at the last minute and everything is rush-rush. For example, this happens when the project manager does not tell resource managers that team members are becoming available until the day they are released. Or it could include the project manager that knows for three months that a specialist is needed, but only asks for the person the week before. In each case, the other party is surprised by the last minute request and does not have time to adequately prepare.

• Team members don't know what is expected of them. In the prior problem situations, communication problems surfaced between the team and outside parties. However, poor communication also occurs within a project team. Some project managers do a poor job of talking with their own team to explain what they are expected to do. Sometimes, the project manager is not clear on when assignments are due. Sometimes the project manager has a vision of what a deliverable looks like, but does not communicate that to the person assigned until the first attempt comes back wrong. Sometimes the project manager does not communicate clearly and team members spend time on work that is not necessary. Again, all of this causes extra work and extra frustration on the part of the project manager and team members alike.

Project Problem #5 Poor Quality Management

➤ Rework.

- ➤ Higher maintenance and support costs.
- ➤ Client dissatisfaction.
- ➤ Missed deadlines and budget.
- ➤ Poor morale.

What's the Solution?

Some project managers are just poor communicators to begin with. If you think you are in this group, you should look for training or mentoring opportunities to become better skilled. However, in most cases, the problem with communication is not a lack of skills, but a lack of focus. Many project managers see communicating proactively on the bottom of their priority list. When they do communicate, it tends to be short and cryptic, as if they are trying to get by with the minimum effort possible.

The key to communicating is to keep the receiver the focal point – not the sender. Try to think about what the receiver of the communication needs and the information that will be most helpful to him or her. If you are creating a status report, put in all the information necessary for the reader to understand the true status of the project, including accomplishments, issues, risks, scope changes, etc. If you are going to need a resource in the future, communicate proactively with the resource manager as early as possible. Then, keep reminding him or her of the need as the time gets closer. For the most part, if you ever surprise someone, it is a sign that you are not communicating effectively. (The only exception is when the project manager is also surprised.) The project manager should also communicate clearly with their team. If you find people are confused about their end-dates or if they are doing work they don't need to do, think about whether you communicated with them effectively.

Define and Plan the Recovery Project

When a project is troubled, usually an outside party is brought in to help with the recovery. This does not have to be a person from an outside company, just someone that is outside of the project already. An outsider is brought in because the problems on the project are usually bigger than the current project manager realizes, or they are bigger than the current project manager can handle. After all, if the project manager could solve the problem or had ideas to turn the project around, he or she should have done so already.

Potential Results of the Recovery

By definition, troubled projects have major problems. In fact, the problems may be too severe to overcome. There are a number of potential scenarios that will result from trying to remedy a troubled project.

The project is turned around and completes successfully (within tolerances). This is the best case, but it is normally not possible. If you take over a troubled project that is trending 50% over budget, for instance, you are not normally going to be able to turn it around to a point where you finish in budget (within your tolerances).

• New expectations are set and met. This is a common result of taking over a troubled project. New estimates and expectations are set, and then the team strives to meet the new expectations.

• New expectations are set and missed. This is also a common outcome if the root causes of the original problems are not identified and resolved. This is actually the worst-case scenario, since the company is no better off after the intervention than they were beforehand. It could be that the money spent since the original intervention will be wasted.

• The project will be cancelled. Many troubled projects are just cancelled and the money already spent is basically written off. This can occur at the point the project is validated to be in trouble or after the new expectations are set. The business value obtained by the original project estimate may not be there at a higher cost.

Of course, there are other permutations. For instance, the project expectations may get reset and missed, and then reset again. The project may be mandatory and need to be completed regardless of the number of missed expectations.

Plan, Then Act, then Check / take feedback from Customer, retrospective & improve

The normal tendency for a person arriving on a troubled project is to jump in with both feet to determine causes and plans for a turnaround. If the project is small, you may be able to do just that. However, if a project is small, you are not typically going to go through the effort of a project turnaround.

Let's assume that the project is big enough to require a formal project turnaround. Rather than just jumping in, the first thing that needs to happen is to recognize that the work to recover the troubled project is itself a project. The recovery project has a start and an end, resources, deliverables, etc. It fits all of the classic definitions of a project. Since it is a project, the first thing that needs to happen is a definition and planning process, just as described in the Ten Step Project Management

Process in steps 1 and 2. Just as with a normal project, you need to look at the characteristics of the recovery project to determine the level of effort required. If the recovery project is a medium-sized project, an Abbreviated Project Definition and a short work plan may be perfectly fine. However, if the project is tens of millions of dollars, the recovery project itself may be substantial and a full Project Definition and work plan should be developed and approved. Just as with a regular project, the definition and planning process gives you a chance to validate:

• The purpose of the recovery project (overview and objectives)

• The deliverables to be produced (scope)

• The other aspects of scope including validating the organizations, the portions of the project to recover, etc.

• The sponsor, project manager and other key stakeholders of the recovery project (project organization)

• The estimated duration and cost of the recovery project

• The assumptions and risks associated with the recovery project, and how the risks will be managed

• Who will be involved in the recovery project (project organization?)

• How the current project will proceed (or will it?) while the recovery project is underway (approach)

Once the recovery project has been defined and planned, the sponsor and appropriate stakeholders should approve the Project Definition. The project manager then needs to manage the recovery project tightly using steps 3 - 10 of the Ten Step Project Management Process. The project manager must focus on the agreed upon work and ensure that the expectations are met. The entire situation will be exacerbated if the recovery project itself is not completed successfully.

Assess the Troubled Project

Once the recovery project has been defined and planned (and approved) the first step is an assessment of the troubled project. This would be equivalent to the Analysis Phase that is typically done at the start of a project.

Verify the Background and Facts

The person performing the assessment may or may not have any background on the project. In many cases, he or she is an outside party that has good assessment and recovery skills, but he or she may not have any specific background on the project itself. When you are performing the assessment, no initial assumption is safe from scrutiny.

Everything about the project should first be validated.

As a part of the initial briefing, you are likely to talk with the sponsor or other senior managers. They will certainly brief you on the background and the problems. However, they are just one voice that you will need to listen to. Even information that comes from the sponsor should be validated and confirmed by others before the assessors make any decisions.

Consult with All Relevant Stakeholders

Some recoveries focus on the project team to determine where the problems lie. However, that is too narrow of a group for the assessment. The project team typically does not see the entire picture, and they may be biased in their understanding of the causes of the trouble. To be effective, the assessment must include:

- Project team

• Sponsor

• Client managers

• Users

• Vendors, suppliers and other third parties that have a high degree of involvement.

Assessing all the major stakeholders will not only allow you to see a more balanced view of the project, but will also help you in implementing the recovery plan. People tend to respond better to adversity and change if they think they have been consulted and had input into the recovery process.

Perform the Assessment

You should have a plan of attack for conducting the assessment. The overall approach for the assessment should have been laid out in the Project Definition for the project rescue, and an initial work plan should be in place.

However, the assessment is going to utilize communication skills and problem solving skills. You can review more information about the communication skills required in the Lifecycle Step Project Lifecycle Process at www.lifecycle-step.com/411.1RequirementsElicitation.htm.

The recovery plan will also take good problem solving skills. It is important to identify the root causes of problems. If there are multiple problems (and there usually are), you need to determine which problems are the most urgent to resolve. You can review more about problem solving techniques at:

• Manage Issues / Cause and Effect Analysis

• Manage Issues / Root Cause Analysis

• Manage Issues / Pareto Analysis

Common Causes

It is true that every project is unique, with a set of unique circumstances that cause problems. However, it is also true that there are some generalities that can be used to guide the assessment in the search for root causes. They are as follows:

· **Up-front Project Definition**

> o Unclear and differing expectations for the objectives of the project

> o Unclear or differing expectations of the scope and deliverables of the project

> o Major risks were missed or were thought to be initial assumptions

> o Lack of strong and clear ownership and sponsorship of the project

> o Not including all of the major stakeholders in the project

> o Making the project too large or too complex through its definition instead of breaking it into smaller pieces

> o Poor upfront estimates for cost and duration

· **Project work plan**

> o Project activities are not broken down into a finite enough level

> o The critical path is not identified and managed

> o The project team doesn't always know what to work on

> o Work is assigned to team members that do not have the proper level of experience and skills

· **Ongoing project management**

o Generally not following good project management and lifecycle processes

o The work plan is not being managed

o Scope is not being managed effectively

o Issues are not being resolved in a timely manner and the delay is adversely impacting the project

o Communication between the client and project team has broken down or is inadequate

o Project risks are not being managed

o Project risks are not being re-evaluated

o The project is not following organizational standards, guidelines and policies.

o The team is not held accountable for missed deadlines

o The resources to complete the project successfully as defined in the Project Definition are not available as needed

o There is not a common understanding of the acceptance criteria of the major deliverables.

· **People and skills**

o The team or client-team relationships are dysfunctional

o Interpersonal and diversity problems among a multi-cultural project team

o The team or the client experiences turnover of key resources

o The project manager does not have the skills required to manage the project (He or she may have good general skills, but not for a project with these characteristics.)

o The team does not have the right skills to complete work within expectations (technical, professional or business skills).

· **Analysis and business requirements**

o Failure to define the requirements is resulting in building the wrong features and functions

o Failure to define requirements clearly and completely leaves major gaps in meeting client expectations.

o The needs of all stakeholders were not considered in the requirements, including users, management and the sponsor

o New requirements are not being managed (scope management problems).

· **Design and technology**

o New or state of the art technology causing unanticipated problems

o Poor solution design causing missed requirements and rework

o Not having the right skills on the project.

· **Construction and testing**

o Requirements and other aspects of scope are not frozen to allow the project to drive toward completion

o Technology components do not fit together as designed

o Poor initial testing techniques cause repeated errors and rework in later tests.

· **Implementation**

o Inadequate training of the solution users

o Implementation fails and a recovery plan is not in place

o Poor overall testing causes major errors that keeps the project team in place longer than expected.

Of course, there are other causes as well - some major and some minor. The assessment may point our one major root cause of the project being troubled, but it is more likely that a troubled project will have a number of major and minor root causes identified.

Develop a Recovery Plan

It is hard to describe a generic process for developing a recovery plan because the recovery plan itself is based on the specific root causes that you come up with during the assessment. If the cause has to do with poor initial estimates, the recovery plan will include re-estimating the remaining work. If the problem is associated with having the wrong skills on the team, the recovery plan will be different.

Identify Alternatives and a Recommendation

After the assessment is complete, a list of alternatives should be developed along with a recommendation. The alternatives will vary greatly, depending on the causes that were uncovered during the assessment. However, a couple of alternatives will normally always be considered:

· Stop the project: If a project is in bad enough shape that a rescue is required, the team should always leave open the possibility that the project should just be cancelled. There are many reasons that cancellation may be the best approach. The product being produced may have missed its window of opportunity in the market, the team may not have the right skills and the organization may not have the right people available to replace them, or the sponsoring organization may have more important priorities now. Of course, a big reason for cancellation is that the business proposition may not be valid any more. A project that made sense at a certain cost may no longer make sense if the revised cost estimate is 50% higher or more.

Sometimes there is a hesitancy to cancel a project because of the implication that all of the money spent so far will have been wasted. However, you should look instead at the money already spent as being a "sunk" cost. Sunk costs refer to money already spent on the project. For the most part, sunk costs represent money that you will never get back. The question in a troubled project is not so much the sunk costs as it is the remaining costs and whether the project makes business sense if you spend the estimated cost to complete the project. If the estimated cost to complete the project, plus the sunk costs, means that the project no longer makes business sense, the project should be canceled. This is generally true even if you have already spent 50% or more of the revised cost. If the project no longer makes business sense, you don't want to be in a position of spending more money on it. It would be better to take the remaining project costs, even if they are 50% or less, and apply that money to an effort that does have business value to the company.

• Let the project continue as is: In some cases, the sponsor may determine that the cost of a project rescue is not worth pursuing.

For example, a project may be projected to complete at a budget 50% higher than estimated. However, the assessment may determine that a cause is that the project cost was underestimated. In this case, there is not much that can "rescue" the project. The sponsor is forced to accept the higher cost of the project, cancel the project or scope back the deliverables. In another example, a project may take 50% longer than originally estimated. However, the project may have had some delays in getting resources on board, meaning the project costs are trending within tolerances. The client may decide to live with the later deadline and decline any radical intervention at this time.

Other alternatives: There are many other common alternatives for rescuing a troubled project. Remember that you may not be trying to get the project to complete within its original deadline and budget. At this point, you may have to settle for a more expensive final cost and a later delivery date.

o **Adding resources to apply extra effort:** Adding resources may be required to complete the project within a reasonable timeframe. This may well increase the project budget. Remember that there is a diminishing return from adding resources. If you have a team of five people and then add one more, you will not get a 20% increase in work. There is start-up time and cross-training involved that will not only take the time of the new resource, but existing team resources as well. You will also find an increase in communication, an increase in team misunderstandings, rework, confusion, etc. Obviously you will get some productive work done as well, but not to the extent you might think. Therefore, you may only get a 15% increase in total work produced. If you added a second resource to the team, the incremental gain may be only 12%. A third resource might gain 8%, etc. You will quickly come to a point where adding more resources actually ends up with the activity taking up more time than it would have if fewer resources were used.

o **Adding resources to apply extra skills:** You may need to add resources with a necessary level of expertise or skill. These people could be experienced consultants that are added for the short term to complete some activities that the current project team does not have the right level of expertise to complete.

o **Paying overtime:** You may recommend that the current team work paid and unpaid overtime to meet a new deadline. If you are paying for the overtime, this alternative may cost the project more money.

o **Offering incentive bonuses:** You can offer incentives for team members, contractors and suppliers to get their work completed in a more aggressive timeframe.

o **Purchasing tools:** You may need new tools to accelerate the schedule. These will usually cost money, and you may have to invest in a learning curve, but you think there will be a payback over the remaining length of the project.

o **Improving processes:** Many of the root causes of project problems need to be resolved through process improvements. If you are working on a small project, there may not be enough time to make process improvements before the project ends. However, larger projects (the kind like this one that need to be rescued) usually have enough time remaining to make process improvements to help turn the project around.

o **Building team dynamics:** If you have root causes that point to team cohesion, you may need to invest in team building activities to get the team working together (again). This team building can also extend to the client and the sponsor. On many troubled projects, there is friction between the client and the project team, and this situation needs to be resolved before the project can get fully on track.

If the project is not cancelled or allowed to continue as is, there are a myriad of options to follow depending on the root causes of the problem. Although the actual recovery alternatives will be different for each project, there are a couple things to keep in mind.

• Make sure you understand the tradeoffs of cost, duration and scope (quality). In many cases, a troubled project will have problems in more than one of these triple constraints. A project that is trending way over budget, for instance, is also probably trending way over schedule as well. The alternatives for recovery should address both sides. That is, you may have an alternative that attempts to bring both budget and schedule back within expectations. However, you may also have alternatives that cost even more money and deliver more quickly, alternatives that deliver the project sooner and cheaper with less functionality and alternatives that deliver the project less expensively but over a longer timeframe. If you have multiple options like this, the sponsor will have more of an understanding of the tradeoffs associated with turning the project around.

• Look for intervention actions that result in a net savings to the project. A troubled project is already off course in one or more areas of cost, duration, quality, client satisfaction, etc. If you recommend rescue activities, you want to try to make sure that the actions result in a net savings to the project. For instance, if you estimate that the effort to rescue the project is 200 hours, you should make sure that the result of the activities will be a net savings to the project of 200 hours or more from the current trend. Keep in mind the triple constraint tradeoffs as well. You may have to spend extra effort and cost to accelerate the schedule, and that tradeoff may be fine. However, you don't want to be in a position where the cost of intervention results in a net increase from the revised project estimate without intervention. You also don't want the timeframe associated with intervention to result in the project delivering later than without intervention, or the quality to be poorer than where it would be if no intervention takes place. In these instances, the best alternative may be to just let the project complete as is.

Get Sponsor Approval

Ultimately, the sponsor needs to decide on a recovery plan, taking the alternatives and recommendations into account. It is possible that the sponsor may have other ideas, but this will not happen if the sponsor was also consulted as a part of the assessment. If a broad audience was consulted to create the alternatives (including the sponsor), the sponsor will more than likely accept the recommendation.

Reset expectations with a revised Project Definition and Work plan

Once you have sponsor approval on the overall recovery approach, you need to go back and update the original Project Definition and work plan. The Project Definition is the place to reset expectations for the project objectives, deliverables, risks, estimated cost and effort, etc.

Given the state of the project and the original expectations, there will probably be major revisions to the Project Definition. Just as the first time through, the revised Project Definition should be circulated and approved by the project sponsor and the major stakeholders.

The project work plan also needs to be revised based on the changes that were approved. There may be two sets of activities that need to be worked on in parallel - one set to address the root causes of the problems on the project and another set of activities focused on the original project activities. In other words, it may not be possible to stop the previous project activities while the corrective actions are put into place. For some period of time, you may need to do both.

Activate the Recovery Plan

At this point, you have developed alternatives for rescuing the project, and your sponsor has approved a recovery plan. You have also revised the previous Project Definition and had it approved by the sponsor and other appropriate stakeholders. You have created a revised work plan that includes the activities necessary to complete the project within the revised Project Definition.

Now you and the team must execute the work plan. This is going to require much more focus than the team had before. The project manager, project team and client need to understand where the project was and recognize the critical nature of the project recovery plan. There can be no more delays. Everyone associated with the team needs to work under a heightened sense of awareness by:

- Proactively communicating status and managing expectations.

- Resolving issues quickly and cleanly.

- Focusing on the minimum requirements necessary

to meet business needs and keeping scope change requests to an absolute minimum. At the same time, the project team needs to be especially aware of raising all scope change requests through the formal scope change process.

• Ensuring that the right resources are available at the right times.

You do not want to have a recovery plan that is separate from the actual work of the project. So, after the recovery plan is developed, you should determine the specific activities required to activate the recovery plan. These activities should be placed in the project work plan to ensure they get worked on while the rest of the project work is progressing.

Measure and Monitor Recovery Plan

It is critical that proactive monitoring and measurement take place to validate the status of the recovery plan and the project in general. The worst result of a project rescue is that the recovery itself fails. If this happens, not only is the entire project likely to be cancelled, but there may be repercussions for those involved including a loss of credibility, less opportunity in the future, a demotion or even a chance of being fired.

The following elements will be a part of measuring and monitoring the project.

• Proactive communication, including Status Reports, status meetings and managing expectations, is necessary. If the project has a Communication Plan, it should also be revised. Some communication activities that do not provide measurable value may need to be stopped. Other communication activities may need to be included to overcome the credibility damage to the project already.

• Meticulous updating of the project work plan to ensure

it is up-to-date and that it always shows a clear path to completion.

• Track costs, effort hours, rework and project errors.

• Measure client satisfaction with the recovery. This includes sending out short client satisfaction surveys, as well as talking first-hand with the major stakeholders to ensure that their expectations are being met.

If the project does not already have these in place, they need to be added as a part of the recovery plan. If they are already in place, the effectiveness of the processes needs to be validated, and other proactive activities may need to be added as well. Remember that the old processes for monitoring and measuring the work may not have been effective and may have contributed to the project getting into trouble. Stronger monitoring and measuring may be needed as a part of the recovery.

Depending on the duration remaining on the project, this may also be a time when the project manager needs to use techniques for micromanagement. Normally, you might not want to be involved in the team work activities on a detailed basis. However, when you are in a recovery, you may need to keep a close watch and close follow-up on all outstanding work.

2.21. AGILE MANIFESTO AND KEY AGILE PRINCIPLES

2.21.1. Agile Manifesto

Agile Manifesto

We are uncovering **better ways of developing software** by doing it and helping others do it. Through this work we have come to value:

Individuals and interactions over processes and tools
Working software over comprehensive documentation
Customer collaboration over contract negotiation
Responding to change over following a plan

While there is value in the items on the right, we value the items on the left more.

Figure 1.0 : Agile Manifesto

Image Source: AgileAlliance.org

2.21.2. AGILE PRINCIPLES

- Highest priority is customer satisfaction, achieved by the early and continuous delivery of valuable software
- Welcome the changing requirements, even those that arise late in development
- Continuous focus on delivering shippable customer priority deliverables in an iterative and incremental way
- Working software is frequently delivered, from a couple of weeks or months, preference to the shorter timescale
- Throughout the project, the business people and developers must work together
- Projects are built around motivated individuals - support and trust them to get the job done
- Face-to-face conversation is the most efficient and effective method of conveying information
- The working software is the principal measure of progress
- Agile processes promote sustainable development, the ability to maintain a constant pace
- Good design and continuous attention to technical excellence enhances agility
- Simplicity and continuous focus on % of work done rather than % of effort spent by team

- Requirements, best architecture, and design emerge from all self-organising teams
- Frequently reflect, how to improve efficiency

2.21.3. KEY AGILE PRINCIPLES

- Focus on the customer and business value
- Iterative and fast development
- Flexible, adaptive, and continuously improving
- Collaboration and team work
- Empowered and self-directed teams

2.22.   AGILE VALUES

Trust – among the various stake holders (team, Scrum Master, Product owner, Project Manager) plays a vital role in making Agile successful

Respect – Individuals have to respect and consider the opinion of all the stake holders, no matter even if a team member is a Fresher to the team

Openness – Team/Scrum Master should be open to the Management and the Product owner while providing the status updates, highlighting risks (both internal and external risks)

Courage – Team should have the courage to say "NO" to the management if we cannot commit to the delivery with appropriate reasons

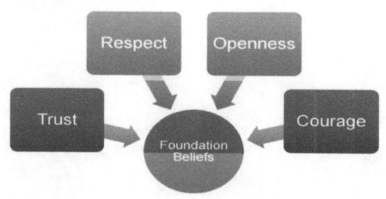

Figure 1.1 : Agile values

2.23. Traditional life cycle vs. Agile Development

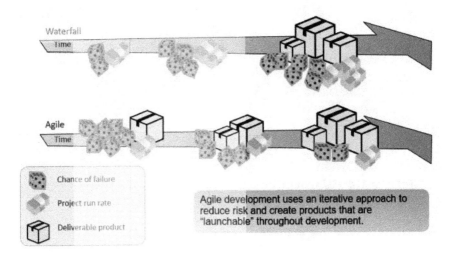

Figure 1.2 : Waterfall vs. Agile

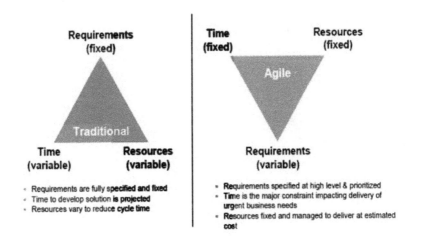

Figure 1.3 : Waterfall vs. Agile – Triple constraints

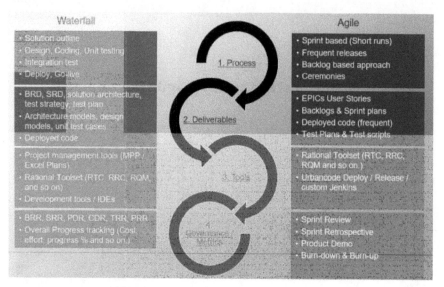

Figure 1.4 : Waterfall vs. Agile – High level comparison

2.24.   AGILITY VERSUS AGILE

Agility

It is the property of an organization to sense and respond to market changes and continuously deliver value to customers.

Agile

An organizational approach and mindset defined by the values and principles of the Agile Manifesto, often practiced through a framework like Scrum.

2.25.   THE STATE
OF AGILITY

A vast majority of organizations recognize the importance of agility and its rewards. Yet agility can be elusive: Many are struggling to translate this nearly 20-year-old software development strategy into a broader management concept. To successfully transform, today's organizations need to embrace agility from strategy to execution, and enterprise-wide.

The time to do so is now. Our survey findings indicate that two-thirds (66%) of organizations have experienced less than 10% growth in revenue over the most recent fiscal year. Trends like this make the ability to react quickly to emerging trends, design better products, enhance team morale, and meet sky-high customer expectations more critical than ever.

Figure 1.5 : The top benefits of organizational agility

Image Source: Forbesinsights

Organizations already recognize the value of agility to the enterprise. A staggering 81% of all survey respondents consider it to be the most important characteristic of a successful organization. And 82% of respondents consider agility to be very or extremely important to an organization's success and competitiveness. Among the most popular Agile approaches selected by respondents: Scrum, cited by more than three-quarters (77%) of leaders.

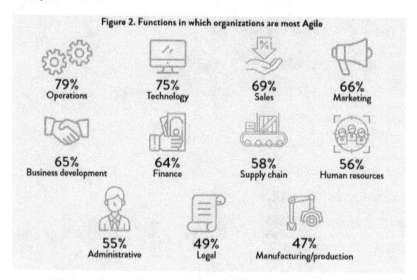

Figure 1.6 : Functions in which organizations are most Agile

Image Source: Forbesinsights

"Agility is a prerequisite to stay competitive in the long run; it is not optional," says Joerg Erlemeier, chief operating officer of Nokia, a Finnish multinational telecommunications and consumer electronics company. "Being Agile enables us to respond faster and better meet our customers' requests." Agile initiatives at Nokia include redesigning business processes, creating a customer-centric supply chain and introducing smaller, more nimble teams.

There's good reason for the popularity of organizational agility. For those that succeed at achieving greater agility, leaders and laggards see many benefits, including faster time to market, faster innovation and improved non-financial results, to name just a few.

Toyota Motor Corporation is just one company reaping the

benefits of increased agility. By working "in small batches" and creating continuous process flows like the Toyota Production System, Nigel Thurlow, chief of Agile for Toyota Connected (the global technology strategy business unit for Toyota), says the company's Kentucky manufacturing plant can upgrade systems that support the plant machinery in six days —a fraction of the seven weeks once required for the exact same task. "When you're working in short sprints and small batches, you're able to see the value delivered more rapidly," he says. "But more importantly, you're able to catch your mistakes more rapidly, change your mind and make decisions based upon emerging requirements."

Such flexibility is imperative in today's business environment, as the rapid pace of technology, innovation and development requires organizations to deliver results faster than ever. But agility is about more than getting products out the door faster than your competitors. Agile began as a response to the failings of traditional software development. Faced with blown budgets and missed deadlines, organizations turned to Agile to increase the rate at which they could create new products and roll out updates.

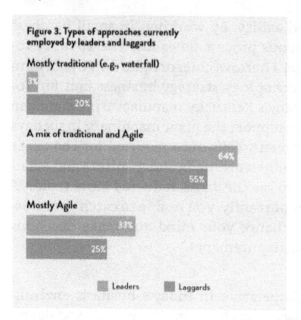

Figure 1.7 : Types of approaches currently employed by leaders and laggards

Image Source: Forbesinsights

2.26. THREE STEPS TO INCREASE AGILITY

1. Create a C-suite with an Agile mindset.

2. Hire and develop the right mix of talent.

3. Foster an Agile-friendly culture and organizational structure.

These strategies enable organizations, many of which are being upended by innovation, to expand agility throughout the organization for sustainable business growth and transformation success.

Solving a client's issue may require many complex work streams, so we set up a sprint...It's a way of getting people to be collaborative, take accountability and feel empowered.

-- TAMARA INGRAM CHIEF EXECUTIVE OFFICER, J. WALTER THOMPSON COMPANY

2.27. AGILE FRAMEWORK

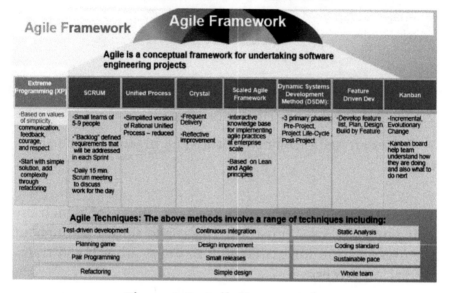

Agile Framework

Agile is a conceptual framework for undertaking software engineering projects

Extreme Programming (XP)	SCRUM	Unified Process	Crystal	Scaled Agile Framework	Dynamic Systems Development Method (DSDM):	Feature Driven Dev	Kanban
-Based on values of simplicity, communication, feedback, courage, and respect -Start with simple solution, add complexity through refactoring	-Small teams of 5-9 people -"Backlog" defined requirements that will be addressed in each Sprint -Daily 15 min. Scrum meeting to discuss work for the day	-Simplified version of Rational Unified Process – reduced	-Frequent Delivery -Reflective improvement	-interactive knowledge base for implementing agile practices at enterprise scale -Based on Lean and Agile principles	-3 primary phases: Pre-Project, Project Life-Cycle, Post-Project	-Develop feature list, Plan, Design, Build by Feature	-Incremental, Evolutionary Change -Kanban board help team understand how they are doing and also what to do next

Agile Techniques: The above methods involve a range of techniques including:		
Test-driven development	Continuous integration	Static Analysis
Planning game	Design improvement	Coding standard
Pair Programming	Small releases	Sustainable pace
Refactoring	Simple design	Whole team

Figure 1.8 : Agile Framework

Agile methodology encourages the continuous iteration of advancement and testing during the project software development life cycle.

Following are some Agile frameworks that can be implemented within Agile projects:

1. Extreme programming
2. Crystal methodologies
3. Scrum
4. Lean software development

5. Feature driven development
6. Dynamic software development methods

Extreme programming is the successful method of developing Agile software. It focuses on customer satisfaction.

To develop the software, extreme programming requires maximum interaction with customers.

It divides the entire software development life cycle into short growth sequences.

2.28. AGILE CONCEPTS

The core ideas in Agile:

Adaptive: The process and the team must be flexible.

Iterative: Agile Development introduces efficient products in stages, which are evolving sets of "completed and working software".

People-oriented: The organisation should support teams and people as they are an essential element for the success of a project.

2.29.   BENEFITS OF AGILE

- Speed to market
- Right Product
- Quality
- Flexibility
- Transparency
- Risk Management
- Cost Control

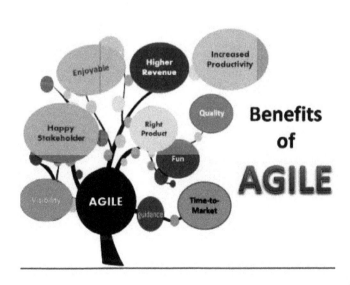

Figure 1.9 : Benefits of Agile

Image source: https://www.prepaway.com/

Agile training and certification helps practitioners to enhance their skill sets by interaction.

2.30.   TECHNICAL BEST PRACTICES

The following are some technical best practices to be followed:

- Test-driven development
- Continuous refactoring
- Automated builds and continuous integration
- Collective code ownership
- Frequent design and code reviews
- Automated acceptance and regression tests

2.31. TEST DRIVEN DEVELOPMENT

This flow chart describes the process followed for test-driven development.

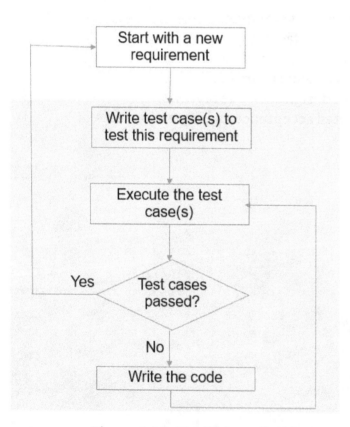

Figure 1.10 : Test driven development

2.32.
ADVANTAGES
OF TEST DRIVEN
DEVELOPMENT

The following are some advantages of test-driven development:

- Makes the developer **first think** about **"how to use"** the component and **only then** about **"how to implement"**
- There is no code without a TEST; thus ensures all requirements are tested
- Greater level of confidence in the code
- Wide test coverage eliminates defects in the early stage
- Increased code coverage

2.33. TOOLS OF TEST DRIVEN DEVELOPMENT

Specific tools are available to support test-driven development.

- Framework for automating the unit tests
  - Example: Junit, JMeter
- Integrated development environment (IDE)
  - For writing tests, using auto-completion and generation of missing code
  - For running the tests
  - For refactoring
    - Example: Eclipse, RAD (Rational Application Developer)
  - Build environment
  - For executing tests automatically and during the build process
  - For computing code coverage
  - For generating test reports
    - Example: Maven, Jenkins.

2.34.   CODE REFACTORING

Code refactoring is the process of restructuring existing code without affecting its functionality.

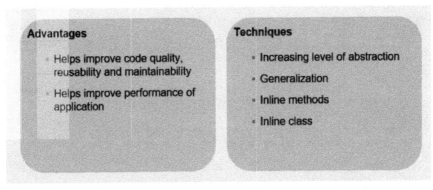

Figure 1.11 : Code refactoring technique

2.35.   SCRUM PHASES AND PROCESSES

Scrum Phases and Processes

Initiate	Plan & Estimate	Implement	Review & Retrospect	Release
Create Project Vision	Create User Stories	Create Deliverables	Demonstrate and Validate Sprint	Ship Deliverables
Identify Scrum Master & Stakeholder(s)	Estimate User Stories	Conduct Daily Standup	Retrospect Sprint	Retrospect Project
Form Scrum Team	Commit User Stories	Groom Prioritized Product Backlog		
Develop Epics	Identify Tasks			
Create Prioritized Product Backlog	Estimate Tasks			
Conduct Release Planning	**Create Sprint Backlog**			

Figure 1.12 : SCRUM phases and processes in a nutshell

2.36. SCRUM FLOW

Scrum Flow

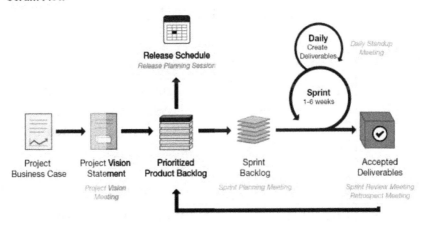

Figure 1.13 : SCRUM Process Flow in a nutshell

2.37.   MOSCOW PRIORITIZATION TECHNIQUE

Letter	Stands for	Which means
M	Must Have	<ul><li>Minimum set of essential requirements, without which the system would be useless (MMF)</li><li>All of these requirements must be satisfied.</li></ul>
S	Should Have	<ul><li>Important requirements for which there is a short-term work-around. The system is useful without them.</li><li>These requirements can be included in the initial project scope, but may be removed from the project scope to accommodate changed requirements.</li></ul>
C	Could Have	<ul><li>These requirements are valuable and nice-to-have, but can easily be left out of the solution.</li></ul>

		■ These requirements may be left out of the initial scope of the release in order to accommodate a time constraint.
W	Would Have/ Won't have	■ Time-permitting ■ As changes to requirements or project progress dictates, lower priority requirements may be removed from the scope of the project.

2.38.   THREE TYPES OF SCRUM TEAM

Type 1: Groups that try to do Scrum

Most Dangerous

- Low-level of task interdependence.
- Do not need to work together as a team (Context does not require teamwork).
- Forced to do Scrum because that is what everyone else is doing.
- Group members hate Scrum because it does not work. How could it?
- Retrospectives add little to no value—Take seven random people in a bar and have them conduct a retrospective on the work they did not do together.

Vital Flaw: Thinking that method precedes context.

Sports analogy: Wrestlers

Type 2: Scrum "Teams"

Characteristics

- People who have a high-level of task interdependence but do not know how to work together as a team.
- They do Scrum things and worry about buffer, writing user stories, and happiness metrics.
- Think sending an email builds situational awareness and is part of closed-loop communication.
- Spend time talking about the differences between themes, initiatives, epics, and stories.
- Retrospectives change frequently and tend to focus on what went well, what didn't, and so on.
- Planning sessions and the daily Scrum look nothing alike.
- Members and coaches hold several certifications and use phrases such as: *That's not agile* and *Let's self-organize and move these chairs toward the wall so we can...*
- Lacks agility but claim they are agile.
- Managers in the organization consider the team to be *Agile* because they are either (1) trained in Scrum or (2) are doing Scrum.
- Have a *me* attitude.
- Low-level of employee engagement.
- May occasionally achieve a 2X improvement in velocity.

Vital Flaw: Assumption that people with high-technical skills or advanced education know how to team.

Sports Analogy: 2002-2004 USA Men's Basketball Dream Team (**Hint**: they lost to teams that knew how to play together)

Type 3: Teams that use Scrum
Significant Competitive Advantage

Characteristics

- Two or more people who work interdependently, adaptively, and dynamically towards a shared and valued goal/objective/mission (This is actually the definition of a team)
- Improve team interactions daily
- Know how to mitigate cognitive biases
- Each member can lead any event
- Members display fallibility
- Prioritized Teamwork training over Framework training (Scrum)
- Practice closed-loop communication
- Challenge each other's assumptions
- Detect weak signals
- Have a *we* attitude
- Scrum used to help prioritize work, build a cadence, and create a container
- Scrum is a force multiplier
- Teams know how to separate decisions from outcomes
- Follow the 60/40 rule in retrospectives: 60% focus on teamwork (Teaming skills) and 40% on task work
- Not uncommon to see a 4X to 16X improvement in velocity

Vital Flaw: Waiting! Waiting is failure!

Sports Analogy: All Blacks, New England Patriots, 1980 USA Men's Olympic Hockey Team.

Bottom line: If you want to create agility, prioritize Team-work over Frameworks.

Give more stress on team outcome achieved rather than efforts spent.

2.39.
CHARACTERISTICS OF SUCCESSFUL PROJECTS

Select highlights from that report as items that are listed as essential or important for project success include:

- Sponsors know what they need and can afford.

- There is a senior project champion within the owner's organization.

- Project managers are experienced professionals dedicated to success.

- Contracts are clear and unambiguous.

- Accountability of project is understood.

- Owner's requirements and expectations are clearly understood.

- Project organization and mission are clearly understood.

- Depth, stability, and time commitments by key personnel are appropriate.

NOTES

Sudipta Malakar

NOTES

3   CHAPTER 3 – CASE STUDY

Case study 1 - A developer's typical day

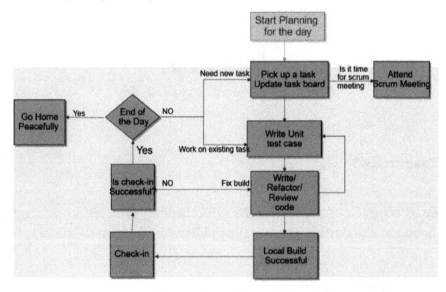

Figure 3.1 : A developer's typical day

Case study 2 - A tester's typical day

Sudipta Malakar

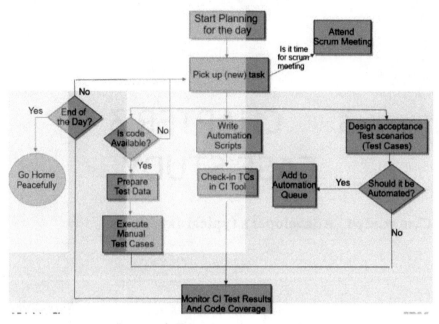

Figure 3.2 : A tester's typical day

Case study 3 -

Case study: software failure - Technical problems causing havoc at the banking group (Royal Bank of Scotland)(2012).

Problem Description - Customers were unable to access any funds credited to their account for 4-5 days. Also a number of customers were unable to use their online banking tools.

Cause: The problem is related to a software upgrade [RBS boss 2012].

Case study 4 –

Case study: software failure - Bugs cause Asian banking fa-

268

cilities downtime (2011).

Problem Description - Internet banking services were shut down for three days, delays in salary payments worth $1.5 billion (£939 million) into the accounts of 620,000 people and a backlog of more than 1 million unprocessed payments worth around $9 billion (£5.64 billion). More than 5,600 ATM machines going offline for 24 hours.

Cause: The problem is related to a software upgrade.

Case study 5 –

Case study: software failure - Software problem encountered at an airport (2008) in the automated baggage sorting system.

Problem Description - Thousands of passengers were unable to check-in baggage for their flights.

Cause: Breakdown occurred during a software upgrade [Denver International Airport, Calleam Consulting Ltd, 2008].

Case study 6 –

Case study: software failure - Software problem encountered for a large urban school system (2007) in a new ERP payroll system.

Problem Description - At various times since the new system went live the preceding January more than one third of the employees had received incorrect pay checks at various times, resulting in overpayments of $53 million, as well as underpayments.

Cause: The problem is related to a software upgrade. Inadequate testing [Report by the Comptroller, NAO, 2006].

Case study 7 –

Case study: software failure - Siemens computer system (1999).

Problem Description - The U.K. Passport Agency implemented a new Siemens computer system, which failed to issue passports on time for a half million British citizens. The Agency had to pay millions in compensation, staff overtime and umbrellas for people queuing in the rain for passports.

Cause: The Passport Agency rolled out its new computer system without adequately testing it or training its staff. At the same time, a law change required all children under 16 travelling abroad to obtain a passport, resulting in a huge spike in passport demand that overwhelmed the buggy new computer system [Report by the Comptroller et. al., NAO, 1999][Lynn T et. al., 1999].

Case study 8 –

Case study: software failure - NASA Mars Climate Orbiter

(1998)

Problem Description - The Mars Climate Orbiter fired its engines to push into orbit around Mars after a 286 days' journey from earth.

Somehow, the engines fired. But the spacecraft fell too far into the planet's atmosphere, likely causing it to crash on Mars.

Cause: Sensor signal falsely indicated that the craft had touched down (130 feet above the surface). Then the descent engines shut down prematurely. The error was traced to a single bad line of software code.

It was noticed that rather than metric units (Newton's), as specified by NASA [Stephenson et. al., 1999] [Mars Climate Orbiter, NASA, 1999], the software that controlled the Orbiter thrusters used imperial units (pounds of force).

Case study 9 –

Case study: software failure - Space roof (Hartford Coliseum Collapse) (1978)

Problem Description - Just hours after thousands of fans had left the Hartford Coliseum, the steel-latticed roof collapsed under the weight of wet snow.

Cause: The programmer of the CAD software used to design the coliseum incorrectly assumed the steel roof supports would only face pure compression. But when one of the supports unexpectedly buckled from the snow, it set off a chain reaction that brought down the other roof sections like dominoes [MTC 470,2001][Levy et. al.,1992][Delatte et. al., 2009].

Case study 10 –

Case study: software failure - ERP project failure in Jordan

Problem Description - ERP project failure lead to huge loss of capital and unsatisfied client [Ala'a Hawari et. al., 2010].

Cause: There were sizeable gaps between the assumptions and requirements built into the ERP system design, and the actual realities of the client organization.

Case study 11 –

Case study: software failure - Therac-25 (1993)

Problem Description - Canada's Therac-25 radiation therapy machine malfunctioned and delivered lethal radiation doses to patients. This caused the death of many people and left many people critically injured [Delores R. Wallace, 2001].

Cause: Due to Inadequate Software Testing.

Case study 12 –

Case study: software failure - STS-126 (2008)

Problem Description - A software change had inadvertently shifted data in the shuttle's flight software code.

Cause: "In-flight" software anomalies occurred and several automated functions failed [Bergin et. al., 2008].

Based on the case studies discussed above, the major cause of software failures is the lack of effective software testing. Some of the severe failures caused loss of millions of dollars, customers' requirements not been met and loss of lives. These all are due to improper testing while upgrading the software, inappropriate testing in various client environments, system testing, integration testing not done efficiently and various other software glitches. The causes have been identified as a part of software testing, as testing is the last check point before releasing the product.

NOTES

Sudipta Malakar

NOTES

4 CHAPTER 4 – A SCALED-AGILE WAY OF BUILDING SOLUTIONS WITH SAP SOLUTION MANAGER 7.20 – NUTS AND BOLTS

4.1. SAP SOLUTION MANAGER 7.2 KEY VALUE CHAINS

Solution Manager is the tool for Application Lifecycle Management and for Service and Support to help customers building and running SAP solution landscapes.

SAP tools and solutions are supporting project teams to build the target business processes from Requirement to Deploy (R2D).

SAP is providing SAP Solution Manager 7.2 plus Focused Build as a preconfigured agile approach to build solutions in an on premise or hybrid landscape.

SAP Solution Manager optimizes digital business transformation.

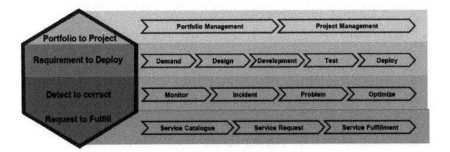

Figure 4.1 : SAP Solution Manager 7.2 key value chains

Image Source: SAP SE / AG

Build with SAP Solution Manager Portfolio-to-project and requirement-to-deploy

1. For SAP and non-SAP:

Covers SAP Business Suite, S/4HANA, Concur, Ariba, Success-Factors and non-SAP solutions

2. On-premise, Cloud, Hybrid:

Supports functional tests for on premise, cloud and hybrid solutions

3. Integration

Seamlessly integrates with all capabilities, supports waterfall and agile development approaches, including Enterprise DevOps

4. All under one roof

No integration setup and ongoing data replication required.

a. Plan & Control

- ➢ Build Project Management
- ➢ Financial Project Management
- ➢ Effort Planning & Time recording
- ➢ Resource Management
- ➢ Work Break Down Structure
- ➢ Project reporting

b. Design & Build

- ➢ Graphical modelling
- ➢ Process management
- ➢ As-is, reference, and to-be landscapes
- ➢ Connection to run-time and design-time
- ➢ Requirements management
- ➢ Solution Readiness Dashboard

c. Test

- ➢ Manual Tests
- ➢ Automated Tests for SAP
- ➢ Test automation framework
- ➢ Test Data
- ➢ Change Impact Analysis
- ➢ Test Planning
- ➢ Test Analytics

d. Deploy

- ➢ Transport control
- ➢ Change traceability

> ➢ Deployment management
> ➢ Release planning
> ➢ Retrofit
> ➢ Quality gate management
> ➢ Change Analytics & Diagnostics

Benefits:

Using SAP Solution Manager in SAP projects is leveraging some crucial delivery success factors:

– Reduced time to value by using Best practices content and processes (Activate & Modell Company)

– Improve efficiency by automation repetitive tasks

– Standardized Delivery for quick on-boarding

– Assured quality with controlled project activities

– Better Predictions by real time project transparency

– Higher Customer satisfaction through early results and agile adoptions

– Seamless transition to operations with one platform to support the SAP application lifecycle.

4.2. SAP SOLUTION MANAGER 7.2 – INNOVATE, ENHANCE, FIX

Three different change paces in requirement-to-deploy.

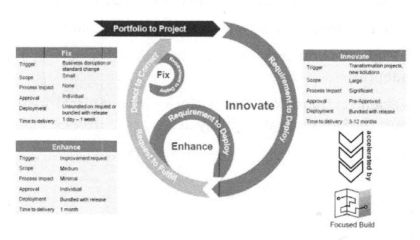

Figure 4.2 : Portfolio Management using SAP Solution Manager 7.2

Image Source: SAP SE / AG

4.3.   FOCUSED BUILD IN A NUTSHELL

Focused Build for SAP Solution Manager 7.2 as tool, together with SAP Activate as methodology, perfectly support you in innovation projects such as SAP S/4HANA implementations.

Focused Build enables SAP Solution Manager for projects.

Focused Build:

➢   Is an add-on solution for SAP Solution Manager 7.2 containing pre-configurations for agile project usage.
➢   Enables you to jump-start SAP Solution Manager for your innovation project.
➢   Provides best practice content, workflow-supported methodology for all project phases and project transparency about all activities.
➢   Requires license per user OR activation via services for Premium customers

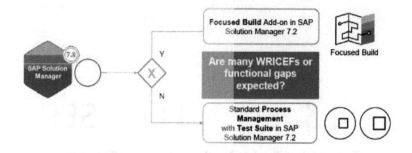

Figure 4.3 : Focus build using SAP Solution Manager 7.2

Image Source: SAP SE / AG

SAP Activate & SAP Solution Manager for on-premise

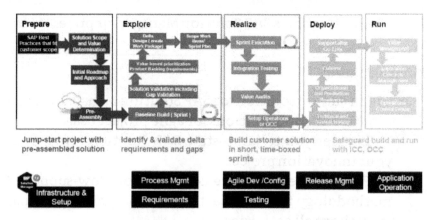

Figure 4.4 : SAP Activate using SAP Solution Manager 7.2 in a nutshell

Image Source: SAP SE / AG

The advantages: accelerating delivery of outcomes.

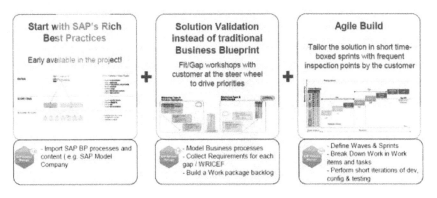

Figure 4.5 : Advantages of SAP Solution Manager 7.2

Image Source: SAP SE / AG

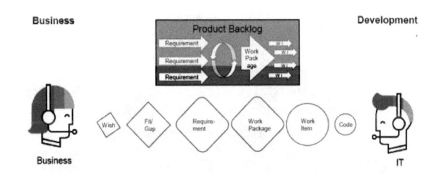

Figure 4.6 : Product backlog in Focused Build

Image Source: SAP SE / AG

Agile project execution and benefits

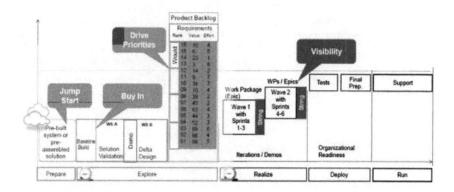

Figure 4.7 : Agile projects execution using SAP Activate Methodology

Image Source: SAP SE / AG

SCRUM methodology – leading agile approach

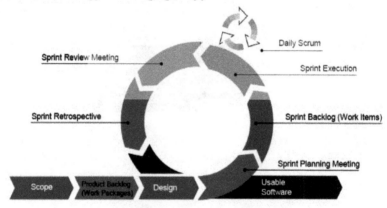

Figure 4.8 : Agile projects execution using SCRUM Methodology

Image Source: SAP SE / AG

Agile and DevOps both boost "time to value".

Agile is a synonym for the "Ability to change efficiently".

Main focus is "collaboration"

> ➤ Fast prioritization
> ➤ Fast team decisions
> ➤ Direct cross communication (Business and Development).

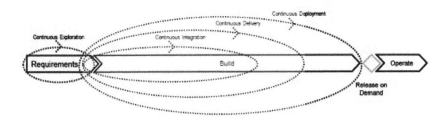

Figure 4.9 : DevOps Methodology high level overview

Image Source: SAP SE / AG

DEVOPS is a synonym for the "Level of automation".

Main focus is "tool automation".

> ➤ Standardized procedures
> ➤ Automation
> ➤ Integrated tool chain
> ➤ But also: ongoing shared responsibility (Dev and Ops).

Why Agile Development and DevOps?

Increase productivity and innovation capabilities in complex environments across all layers.

DevOps as agile approach to bridge the gap between development and operations to deliver value faster and more reliable.

SAP Solution Manager

➤ SAP Solution Manager with Focused Build provides support for agile software development.

➤ The lifecycle capabilities of SAP Solution Manager provide support for build & run (including automatization)

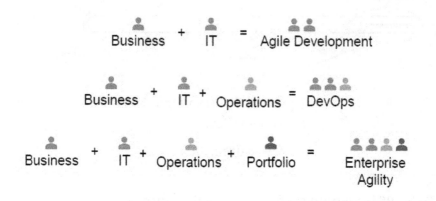

Figure 5.0 : DevOps Methodology high level overview

Image Source: SAP SE / AG

Together this serves as a tool foundation for DevOps.

4.4. PROCESS FLOW FOCUSED BUILD REQUIREMENTS-TO-DEPLOY

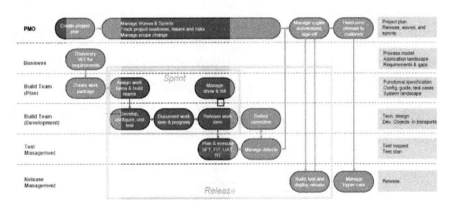

Figure 5.1 : Process flow of SAP focused build requirements

Image Source: SAP SE / AG

Why Project Managers love to start their projects with Focused Build?

1. The demand to realize processes that are fulfilling all business process requirements in time and budget.

2. Starting with Best Practices of content but not with a blank piece of paper and guidance of any task in software projects?

3. Immediate available tool to quickly enable the project team with standardized and agile processes on a high degree of usability.

4. Transparency on current project status to react early on any exception and ability to manage distributed project teams.

5. Efficient processes in project activities which reduces efforts and avoids data disruption.

4.5. EFFICIENT DEVOPS AND SCALED AGILE WITH FOCUSED BUILD

Incremental deployment with constant feedback loops with the business.

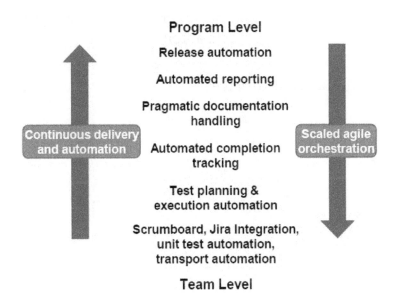

Figure 5.2 : Scaled Agile with DevOps with SAP focused build

Image Source: SAP SE / AG

➤ Releases synchronize project go lives and ensure continuous delivery and integration.

➤ Project to bundle deliverables. Multiple and parallel projects are possible

➤ Phases ending with Quality Gates. Short prepare and scope, incremental build

➤ Waves ending with Acceptance by the business (~ 8 –12 weeks)

➤ Sprints with Show and Tell sessions to the business (~ 2 weeks).

Scaled Agile -SAFe® 4.5

A comprehensive software lifecycle concept - not only for tomorrow.

Scaled Agile SAFe® is a comprehensive concept to scale agile collaboration up through different enterprise levels – cross IT and Business.

Aim is to maximize 'time to value'.

Figure 5.3 : Scaled Agile at different levels with SAP focused build

Image Source: SAP SE / AG

Some advantages are:

➤ IT-Solution is driven by business
➤ Prioritization is driven by business
➤ Program Increments (every 6 weeks) ensure fast 'Time to Value'
➤ Strong collaboration cross IT and Business
➤ Continuous Delivery built in
➤ Not tool bound.

4.6.   FOCUSED BUILD FOR SAP SOLUTION MANAGER 7.2

SAP Solution Manager 7.2 incl. Focused Build solutions are now available in the SAP Cloud Appliance Library (CAL).

SAP provides the powerful appliance without SAP CAL charges. Customers and partners only need an Amazon Web Services (AWS) account to test drive the SAP Solution Manager cloud appliance for as a free trial.*

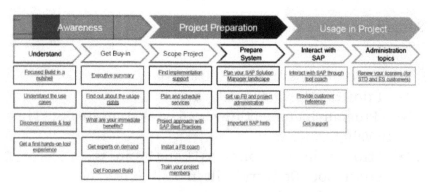

Figure 5.4 : SAP Solution Manager 7.2 high level overview with SAP focused build

Image Source: SAP SE / AG

References –

https://wiki.scn.sap.com/wiki/download/
attachments/467538817/Focused%20Build%20%20How
%20to%20get%20started%201.1.pdf?
version=1&modificationDate=1500467703773&api=v2

NOTES

NOTES

5 CHAPTER 5 – EMPIRICAL ANALYSIS OF RCA FOR SOFTWARE PROJECTS FAILURE – NUTS AND BOLTS – STATISTICAL METHODS

5.1
INTRODUCTION

Root Cause Analysis (RCA) is the process of identifying project issues, correcting them and taking preventive actions to avoid occurrences of such issues in the future. Issues could be variance in schedule, effort, cost, productivity, expected results of software, performance parameters and customer satisfaction. RCA also involves collecting valid data, analyzing it, deriving metrics and finding root causes using RCA methods. In this chapter we will do Root cause analysis of some severe software failures that happened in the past and of some failures in ongoing projects in the software Industry. We will also describe various RCA methods and processes used in the software Industry to reduce the chances of software failure. The Root Cause is defined as the primary cause to any problem, which if found and resolved can solve the problem. Analysis of historical Root Causes should be included in testing and development processes, so that problems of a similar nature do not occur in the future. Root Cause Analysis (RCA) is the process to find out the causes of all deviations during the project life cycle [James J. Rooney et al., 2004] [A D Livingston et al., 2001] [S. Vasudevan et al., 2005] [Mukesh soni et al., 1997] and is done as a corrective as well as preventive action for the deviations. The RCA process should be considered complete when an action plan is prepared and implemented to fix the root causes of software failure, which is generally prepared and implemented by the project managers. Root Cause Analysis will only make sense when proper data collection methods are followed and valid data is gathered by all team members and is finally represented in form of diagrams and figures, so that appropriate actions for root cause analysis can be selected.

The RCA process should be facilitated by a senior member of the team and all the stakeholders should be involved. RCA should be done after completion of every phase of the project, if something is not going well in the project. It is wrong to say that RCA should be done only in case of software failure; it is advisable and necessary to do it after every project release, to discuss all the data outside the control limits in data charts collected for the project [Reising et al., 2007]. If no bugs are found in the project, then there could be a case that the testing team did not do well and if there are excessive bugs in any module then there is a need to analyze the development team issues.

Lessons learnt and root causes identified from all the software failure case studies should be documented. So that all the projects can benefit from them and project teams can take actions to avoid any preventable risks.

5.2   RCA PROCESSES AND METHODS

Root Cause Analysis (RCA) is a method of solving problems from any phase of a process, which affects the project progress or the quality of the overall product.

There are various RCA methods and tools being used across the industry to improve the process and avoid the chances of software failure. Root cause analysis is not a defined methodology but there are many different processes and tools used for performing RCA.

RCA Processes

RCA is performed to make sure that the anomalies that occurred in the current project will not reoccur, by taking necessary preventive actions based on the lessons learnt in the current project. This is one of the most important phases of a project life cycle, where all major stakeholders of the project sit together and discuss the areas which went well, which did not go well and how could they be improved further by taking corrective and preventive actions.

This process would be more effective if everything discussed were documented in appropriate templates and timelines were defined against corrective actions to be taken. A formal methodology should be followed while doing RCA for any problem statement. The processes mainly depend upon the data collected for a particular phase of the project or for the overall project, for which RCA is to be done. The data should be collected properly and reviewed by a senior person on a daily basis. Once the data is validated and entered in the templates, then all the variances are identified and appropriate RCA methods are applied, which is generally done by some facilitator. All stakeholders discuss their points and mention what went well, what did not go well and how the project can be improved.

The facilitator writes down all the points after verifying them with the group, and at the last stage, a preventive and corrective action plan is defined and a timeline is assigned to implement it. Later the facilitator or the auditor reviews the plan and makes sure that all the corrective and preventive action items are implemented and finally the RCA is stored in the organization repository, so that it can be referenced later for future projects.

RCA Methods

There are various well known methods used for performing RCA [Andersen et. Al., 2000].

Most commonly used root-cause analysis methods are:

a. Cause-Effect Analysis: The cause-effect analysis uses fishbone (Ishikawa) diagrams to illustrate how various causes can be linked to an identified effect.

There may be a series of causes that can be identified, one leading to another. This series should be pursued until the fundamental, correctable cause has been identified. The Fishbone diagram technique is used to identify the influencing factors for a number of identified problems within a range of contributory factors.

b. Events and Causal Factor Analysis: Events and Causal Factor Analysis consists of the identification of a series of tasks and/or actions in a time sequence, as well as the environmental conditions of the tasks leading to an incident occurrence. The resulting Events and Causal Factor chart provides a graphical representation of the timeline and relationships of the events and causal factors, including more details than Cause-Effect Analysis.

c. <u>Fault Tree Analysis</u>: Through successive refinements from general to specific FTA provides backward reasoning. It examines preceding events leading to failure in a time-driven relational sequence as a deductive methodology. It is a graphical representation of the potential combinations of failures generating the incident. It starts with a 'top event' representing the analyzed incident. It then decomposes it into contributory events and their relationships until the root causes are identified.

d. <u>Causal Factor Charting (CFC)</u>: In order to describe the events leading to the incident occurrence during investigation CFC analyzes the information gathered as a sequence diagram with logic tests and provides a structure for investigators.

e. <u>Brain Storming</u>: There are two main approaches to Brain Storming: Structured and Unstructured. Structured Brain Storming is where the facilitator asks each member of the group to contribute a suggestion or idea. This is a useful approach, but if some members of the group are very dominant, then this approach makes it difficult for other members to contribute. Unstructured Brain Storming is a free for all. This allows for spontaneity, but can also lead to a loss of ideas. The key to successful brainstorming is to focus on all members contributing their ideas, and not allowing any in-depth questioning or exploration until the process of brainstorming is completed. The facilitator must also be careful to record ideas as they are spoken.

f. The 5 Whys: The 5 whys is a question-asking technique used to find the cause and effect relationship to explain a particular problem. The main goal of this technique is to find root cause of a problem. The technique was originally developed by Sakichi Toyota and was used within the Toyota Motor Corporation during the evolution of its manufacturing methodologies.

5.3 PHASE WISE ROOT CAUSES ANALYSIS OF SOFTWARE FAILURES

Based on our survey of 146 employees from 27 companies, it is evident that software testing including up-gradation, environment issues, cloud related issues and configuration issues are major areas of concern, which need to be focused upon to prevent software failures. Configuration and environmental issues exist because of integration of multiple applications built in various platforms of different domains using web services and other applications. The root causes from all the phases of software failures are explained below, which are collected after a review of literature and from the survey.

5.4 ROOT CAUSES ANALYSIS OF PROJECT PLANNING, REQUIREMENTS AND DESIGN PHASE

Project planning, requirement and design are the primary phases that lay the foundation of the software product. If issues are not found and fixed early in these phases then the cost of fixing them later may increase exponentially. Most of the issues start while gathering and eliciting requirements for the project. In practical scenarios, the requirements of customers keep on changing and never get finalized until the project is completed. This phenomenon introduced agile methodology and created havoc to developers and project management teams, because it is altogether a different approach than the traditional one. Also, at beginning of the project, all domains, technology, management training needs should be gathered and planned effectively. An effective team is the most important asset of any organization, so they should feel motivated throughout the project.

Below are the high-level causes of failures from this phase:

- Incomplete or Improper Requirement Documenta-

tion.
- Change in Requirements not communicated to Development and QA teams.
- Frequent change in requirements and requirement changes allowed near deadlines.
- Change management process not followed.
- Prototypes and Design are not self-explanatory
- No formal estimation technique.
- Estimates not revised when requirements are changed.
- Lack of experience in domain and inappropriate training.

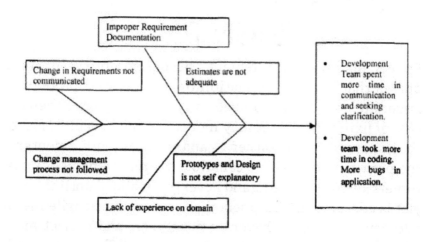

Figure 5.1 : Fishbone Diagram 1: Reflecting the "Cause and Effects of Project Planning, Requirements and Design"

5.5 ROOT CAUSES ANALYSIS OF DEVELOPMENT PHASE

Development phase starts with understanding the requirements, designs and selecting the technology/platform to develop the required system. In mature organizations and CMMi 5 companies; coding standards, guidelines, procedures are followed effectively, however in small and medium companies, this is a major issue. Each and every developer follows his own coding standard, which makes it hard to review and fix the bug and ultimately impacts the maintainability of the system. This is the age of modular and component based systems, where developers reuse the already existing components to support the same. Once these requirements are fixed, the problems arise due to improper check-in and checkout of the code, version controlling and status accounting of the system, which occurs when configuration management tools are not used; or when these tools are used, they are not implemented effectively. One of the most challenging aspects for developers is unit testing of their own code. Developers consider their code as the best code in the world, so they only write for unit tests at a low level, rather than preparing unit test plans, cases, recording results and maintaining logs.

At a high level below are causes of failures from this phase:

- Development team not trained properly on all technologies aspects
- Coding standards not followed
- Configuration Management tool not used or, if used, not used appropriately.
- Development team not performing formal unit testing.
- Developers don't prepare unit test plan, unit test cases, not recording results and maintaining test logs.

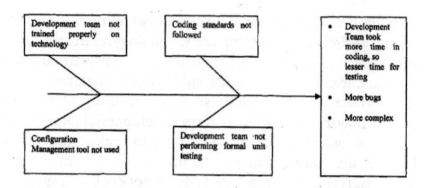

Figure 5.2 : Fishbone Diagram - 2: Reflecting the "Cause and Effects of Development Phase"

5.6   ROOT CAUSES ANALYSIS OF SOFTWARE TESTING AND IMPLEMENTATION PHASE

A lot of work has already been done in this field; however there are still some pain areas in current industry due to intricacies in complex applications integrated with outside world applications and communicating with other technologies. Also at this point of time, there is a diverse customer base working on various environments, which needs to be satisfied by built-in application to sustain in business. This ultimately makes it difficult to test the system for all possible conditions.

Software testing is the most important phase to ensure successful deployment, because there is no major checkpoint after this phase. If a critical bug is not found in this phase and is not fixed, then it could disrupt the overall system. Software testing time is always consumed by the development team and the testing team is left with less time, which leads to lot of issues. There are currently so many functional and performance testing tools, which makes that tool selection is difficult. There are various other traditional issues, which prevail in current industry. For example, review processes are not followed appropriately and all test cases with various data sets are not prepared and executed in all environments and browsers.

At a high level below are causes of failures from this phase:

- Functional testing not done appropriately.
- Performance testing not done at all.
- Testing teams are not properly trained on functional and performance tools
- Look and feel testing not done in all browsers and with all configuration settings.
- Test cases are not prepared for all requirements.
- Test management tools are not used effectively to fully utilize all its features.
- Lack of review process (peer review, internal review, external review).
- Lack of negative testing and test cases.
- Test cases are not updated every time when requirements change.
- Non-availability of various test data sets in test environment.
- Implementation and Up-gradation testing is not done appropriately.
- Environment and configuration issues crop up quite often at client side.

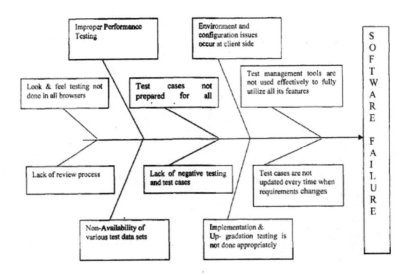

Figure 5.3 : Fishbone Diagram 3: Reflecting the "Cause and Effects Software Testing and Implementation"

5.7   SUMMARY

This chapter presents empirical study of root cause analysis of software failure. In the current scenario, it is really difficult to perform end-to-end testing, where complex systems are integrated with outside world applications, which communicate with each other using multiple interfaces. Now, the software industry is mature enough and most of the software applications are in the maintenance phase. Software application upgrades are done frequently during the maintenance phase. A lot of software applications crash, if testing is not done thoroughly, at the time of software up-gradation. After the empirical study of root causes of software failures, it is also observed that lots of software failed at the time of upgrading the software and due to inadequate system and integration testing. There is minimal testing performed at the time of software up-gradation, which leads to software failures. So a new integrated software testing technique needs to be developed, which would quickly validate the application under test and ensure 100% coverage while upgrading the software. This can be done by having a test suite having minimal test cases ensuring maximum coverage.

NOTES

NOTES

6 CHAPTER 6 – KEY TAKEAWAYS

The methodology used to perform RCA included the following steps:

Step 1 — Define the problem.

Step 2 — Gather data and evidence.

Step 3 — Identify Issues that contribute to the problem.

Step 4 — Find the root causes.

Step 5 — Develop recommended solutions.

Step 6 — Establish milestones and performance measures.

Step 7 — Implement recommended solutions (corrective actions and preventive actions).

Step 8 — Observe and measure performance for desired outcome in XMR / Control chart and measure the effectiveness of implemented CAPA (corrective actions and preventive actions) activities.

By agile, we mean a number of things:

- Enhanced flexibility

- Empowering employees to work where, when and how they choose

- Iterative delivery of projects

- Co-ownership of projects with the client / customer

- The opportunity to adapt ways of working and processes as objectives change and move on throughout a project lifecycle.

Which of these descriptions best applies to the project management function within the organization?

- Established processes in place, with ongoing improvements and innovations introduced, based on feedback from monitoring and evaluation.

Senior managers are actively keen that the Portfolio Program Manager (PPM) function becomes more strategic (e.g. has more tangible and identifiable impact on overall business goals and finances).

Agile is a value driven approach, not plan driven.

A plan driven, project focused, approach is what we learned when we got our PMP's. Everything is planned up front. Requirements are fixed, and cost and schedule are estimated. We then report status based on how the project is doing compared to the plan.

When it comes to software development, we know a plan driven approach is flawed. Yet, many companies continue to use it. Why? Why do we punish project teams for being over budget or behind schedule when we know it's the process that's broken?

We need to shift our mindset from project focus, to product focus.

Product focus is a value driven, adaptive process. It doesn't punish teams for change. It anticipates change and even welcomes it.

In a value driven approach, cost is fixed, and features are estimated. It's the reverse of a plan driven approach. Investment is made at the product level, not a project level. People are dedicated to teams, and the teams stay intact.

This move from project focus to product focus is not pie in the sky. It's not for small tech firms only. Target, for example, has completely shifted to a product focus model. They get it, and they're not alone. Many large companies are organizing cross functional teams around products. They are bringing IT and business people together to focus on delivering business outcomes.

If your company is going Agile, ask yourself, are you ready to move on from traditional project management? Are you ready to no longer have a PMO? Are you ready to change? If yes, then it's time to embrace a product focused mindset. If no, then continue using Waterfall, but don't call it Agile.

Bottom line: If you want to create agility, prioritize Teamwork over Frameworks.

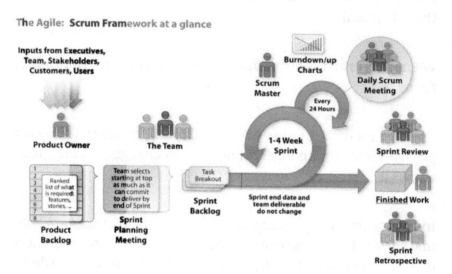

Figure 6.1 : Agile SCRUM Process flow in a nutshell

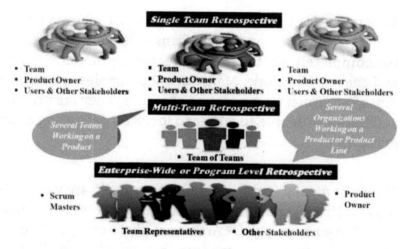

Figure 6.2 : SCRUM Retrospective types

Recovering your project from disaster

Despite the best laid plans, sometimes Program Managers realize that the Project is out of track and need to take some corrective and preventive measures to rescue it from disaster.

NOTE. If you have the time and resources to sit down and come up with a detailed plan – then your project is already a disaster!

It is important to 'think of wide' when considering possible actions to get your project back on track.

A common knee jerk reaction is to throw more staff resource or money at the problem, but that is not always the best thing to do. Indeed, for some problems simply throwing more people into the work just makes matters worse.

A great help is to bring in the team leader and possibly team members to talk about the problem.

It is most often the case that your specialist team members can see solutions, indeed, can help you identify the root causes. After all, if your team are specialist experts, they will bring a wealth of experience and ideas to help implement corrective actions that will work.

Avoid the temptation to micromanage your project schedule and budget, after all if it is just a little off track, the best solution might be to keep things going the way they are but simply fast track the effort for the next few days to get your schedule back.

It's also important not to panic and throw together a hastily thought through action plan without considering the full consequences.

Finding out why the project is off track

When you get a problem, first look at the underlying causes and try to understand the characteristics of the problem.

It is only when you properly understand both the characteristics and the causes of deviations from the plan that you can come up with sensible corrective actions.

If your project goes off track, it probably is not anybody's fault, it is simply that the project is not proceeding the same way as you anticipated on the plan.

You need your team members on board to keep the project momentum going and probably to help solve the problem.

Try using the FIVE 'WHY's

It's human nature. You have a crisis and dive straight into fixing "it" without first stopping to think 'why did it happen?' If you identify the root cause FIRST, then you can identify options to recover the situation.

This is a powerful technique I am teaching in our forthcoming Lean Six Sigma Masterclass that helps identify the root cause of a problem. It is important to first determine the relationship between different root causes of a problem – and so here is a suggested sequence:

> Write down the specific problem, this helps you formalize the problem and encourages you describe it in detail. It also helps everyone focus on the same problem

> Ask "Why" the problem happens and write the answer down below the problem statement

> If the answer you just provided doesn't identify the root cause of the problem that you wrote down, ask Why again and write that answer down

> Repeat until the team agrees that the problem's root cause has been identified. This may take fewer or more times than five Whys.

When carrying out your initial analysis, consider the following:

> Is the project going off track or is it that the project is 'right' and it's the plan that is 'wrong'? In other words, is the plan unrealistic? You may need to adjust the plans for the rest of the project in the light of this experience

> Is this a problem with planned work, or has extra necessary work been discovered that was not anticipated on the plan? This problem is made less likely if you have done proper planning using breakdown structures and

workflow diagrams in the first place.

➢   If you have only done activity planning, then this is
likely the cause of your current problem (check out our
"product-based planning" technique)

➢   Is there a problem because the work requires more
effort than expected, or is the work estimate right and
the problem is that the team members have not been able
to put in the planned time and effort? For example, have
team members been called away and repeatedly to do un-
foreseen operational, non-project, work?

➢   Are the team members going more slowly than expected because of unfamiliarity or inexperience? Would
it help to ask for more experienced staff, or would the
learning curve of new staff getting to understand the project, only makes things worse?

➢   Have the teams been held up because necessary equipment is not available? For example, have delays in other
projects held up the release of equipment that is needed
for this project?

➢   Is the problem because something is more complicated
than anticipated? Does that mean that other products
within this project, will also be more complicated?

➢   Is this a one-off problem that affects only this part
of the work? Or is the problem the first sign that that
everything is going to take longer than expected. In other
words, are the estimates understated throughout the
whole of the project?

➤ Were your assumptions correct? It's quite normal for these to be tweaked as the project progresses. If assumptions need to be adjusted, do it now and update your plan. This may need to be agreed with senior management.

➤ Is the cause of the problem something you can control or is it, by its very nature, outside of your control, such as higher than normal sickness levels due to particularly nasty bug that is circulating?

➤ Is the activity on the Critical path? Delayed activities on the Critical path will delay your overall project schedule. If the activity is on the Critical path, you will need to take more extensive controlled action than if it has spent time (float) that can absolve some or all the delay

➤ Is the activity on a path that is close to being critical? Activities on non-critical parts can have some delays before the pols become critical. The maximum delay for non-critical activities is called slack or float. If the activities float is very short, a small delay can cause that above to go critical

➤ Has the work already been identified as involving risk? If so, have you got some management actions planned already and set down in your risk log. Such actions will normally take time and effort, and so the next thing to check is that such time and efforts have been built into your project schedule Perhaps you set up a risk budget. If you are off track to due to risks that occurred, perhaps you should use that budget to get back on track.

➤ Have you already encountered problems with this activity? Unless new factors have arisen, the recurrent problem suggests that previous controlled actions are not proving adequate.

Something has happened either from within or outside of the project that has truly rocked your boat...

So, my next list of approaches (some to get the project spend back in control, others to redeem the project schedule – or both), may help in that regard:

➤ Can you negotiate a reduction in project scope so that you can still meet important deadlines? Perhaps renegotiate the sequence of key deliverables to meet interim milestones?

➤ Split your delivery project into two 'phases' or tranches. The first to deliver 'must-have' customer prioritized products/services, the second to deliver 'should-have/could-have' products services

➤ Outsource key aspects of the project to a third party. They may have higher skills levels and get things done more swiftly; on the other hand, they may be cheaper/ more expensive. Time/cost priority will dictate here

➤ Hire in contractors to supplement the team to fast-track progress, or again, to use higher skills to speed up the schedule

➤ The Project Approach. If you are designing one or all of your products 'in-house', investigate the option of buying some products 'of-the-shelf' – either as they are, or customizing them in some way. This is the "Make or Buy" approach and should be financially justified.

Taking Corrective Action

If your project is behind in terms of schedule, then check out your Gantt chart and see if there are any tasks coming soon that have available float, in which case you could use that float to bring your project back on schedule.

In a similar way, available float may not be needed, and hence the opportunity arises to slow down the rate of costs, and over a period of time get back within cost budget.

When considering your options for bringing the project back on track, include the following in your thinking:

> Use contingency to absorb an overrun if you are out of float. You should have time, and sometimes cost, contingency in the plan to allow for problems – in which case use it!

> Accept an overrun but 'buy back' some contingency. If the activity is something that you cannot put extra people on, you may have to just accept the overrun, as I've said, it is what the contingency was there for in the first place

> However, if you are unhappy that it has taken up too much of your contingency for this point in the project, you may be able to buy back some contingency time by putting more staff on a later activity and so shortening its duration.

> Split the work. It may be that part of the work must be done now, and although it was preferable that the whole job was completed, in fact some of its can be done later in

parallel with other activities

➤ Shortening an activity, usually by putting more stuff onto its where that would be effective, is called crashing the schedule. It's not a particularly good word because it sounds more like a disaster than a corrective action, but that's what it's called!

Deciding what you will do.

Having considered a range of options for action, now is the time to make your mind up on what action or actions you are going to take. Your decision is likely to revolve around three factors:

➤ What you think will be the most effective
➤ What the cost is likely to be in terms of money and staff time
➤ What the impact will be on other projects.
To determine the last of these factors, your plan must be up to date. Project planning and control tools can help when looking at impacts, because you can do 'what if' projections using the tool.

Remember to save a baseline copy first before you start making changes.

This will also be helpful in comparing such changes against the original plan. It's maybe that you need to run your actions passed your project board to get their approval before implementing.

Implementing Your Actions

Having reached a decision on what to do you must adjust your plans to include those actions and then adjust the work in line with the revised plans.

The implementation may involve talking with others in the project, including individual team members, to explain the problem, what you are doing about it and how it will affect their work.

This will have an added advantage in that your team will be committed to making your revised plan work.

Monitoring the effectiveness of your actions

In some cases, after the controlled action is put into effect, that is the end of the matter. But in many cases, you need to check that your actions are proving effective.

If the actions are working, then fine, but if not, you will need a look at why that is, see what the range of actions are now possible in the light of this new information, choose what to do (going through the above steps for a second time), then monitor again.

Improvement Opportunities

It occurred to me some time back, that in the cut-and-thrust of project management, once a project is underway – while the project manager is monitoring progress (or otherwise!) and controlling by taking action, their seems to be just two situations:

Managing Issues (these are situations that have already emerged or are about to).

Managing risks. (these are situations that have yet to occur – they may or may not occur at some point in the future).

The Risk Twist

But the way our brains are wired, we, the human species are notoriously bad at managing risks.

Now, I do NOT intend to turn this into a risk management training, but in the spirit of project disaster recovery, there is a Lean Six Sigma technique that is particularly powerful when it comes to risk management ...

Let me suppose, you have used all the advice and guidance I have given you thus far, and you are on your way to getting your project out of the quagmire.
Probably, the very reason you got into difficulties in the first place was mediocre project risk management.

I am sure you know all about how to estimate a risk's severity (probability multiplied by its impact).

Considering Risk Proximity

THIS is what us humans are bad at managing!
Proximity defines how soon it can happen and how soon you will be hit by the impact.

Broadly, there are THREE categories that you need to manage to get the full benefit of disaster recovery:

Immediate
Some risks always have a proximity of now and the impact will be immediate. They can happen at any time during the project with no notice at all. An easy example is with a team member going sick.
They may walk up to you in 5 minutes time and say that they are feeling dreadful and needs to go home - or that could happen in five weeks' time or in five months' time.

Fixed date
Some risks are pegged to a point in time. The new rocket cannot fail to launch until it is time to launch it. The team cannot find a product is more complicated to build than they thought, and so will take longer, until they get to grips with the product as they start to build it.

For this category, note that the proximity will get shorter and shorter as you approach the date when the risk can occur.

Fixed Period
The impact of some risks will always be a fixed time ahead. Today the proximity is four weeks, that if the risk occurs in five months' time, the proximity of the impact will be four weeks after that.

Consider the simple example of someone resigning from your organization and so leaving your project. If that person resigns today, they will leave in four weeks' time, after they have worked their four-week notice period.

If they resigned in five months' time, they will leave for weeks after that.

Which brings me to how you need to manage proximity.

The traditional way is to estimate such proximity for each risk and keep that updated in the project Risk Log. Fair Enough.

But that does not help with project disaster recovery – indeed, vital proximity information buried in the Risk Log may have contributed to your current crisis.

CRITICAL THINKING IS A CORE SKILL OF SUCCESSFUL PROJECT MANAGERS

➢ Think back to how project management is applied
➢ Activities, methods, processes, procedures and techniques only go so far

- ➢ Think about planning and monitoring
- ➢ Think about estimating and identifying risk responses
- ➢ Think about project strategies and approaches
- ➢ Think about project controls
- ➢ Think about delivery approaches

ALL the above, and more, depend 100% upon Critical Thinking.

Think You Can Do WITH Critical Thinking…

Critical Thinking Skills and activities for Project Managers Critical thinking is for everyone, yet few are able or willing to do it. Critical thinking is a set of transferable skills that can be learned for one thing yet equally useful for any other.

Critical thinking cuts across all academic disciplines and is applicable in all spheres of human activity - particularly project management where it becomes a toolbox for driving both career and project success.

So what are the key activities, abilities and attributes of a critical thinker?

Analytical skills

Like any one skilled in debate, critical thinkers demand properly constructed arguments that presents reasons and more sound conclusions

Tolerance

Critical thinkers delight in hearing diversion views and enjoy a real debate

Confidence

This is key since critical thinkers must be confident and able to examine views made by others, often those in authority

Curiosity

This is the essential ingredient for ideas and insights

Truth seeking

It is one critical skill which every Program Manager needs to have.

NOTES

Sudipta Malakar

NOTES

7   CHAPTER 7 – SAP HANA BLOCKCHAIN SERVICE

What is Blockchain?

Bitcoin

For verifying the transfer of funds, operating independently of a (central) bank cryptocurrency encryption techniques are used.

Blockchain

Architectural concept that enables the decentralized, secure, direct, digital transfer of values and assets.

Distributed Ledger Technology

Distributed ledger consensus of replicated, shared digital data across various countries, sites or institutions. No central administrator or centralized data storage.

Blockchain is a new protocol for distributed ledgers in multi-party business processes. Blockchain can transform transactional networks.

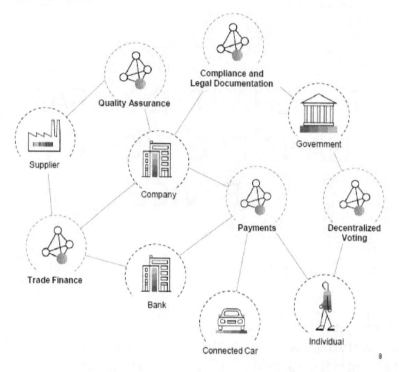

Figure 7.1: Transformation of transactional networks by Blockchain

Image Source: SAP SE / AG

Value Drivers for Businesses

a. Process optimization

Multi-Party collaboration on single version of truth.

b. Time & Cost Reduction

Peer-to-peer network without intermediaries.

c. Transparency & Auditability

Undeniable history due to immutability of records.

d. Risk & Fraud Minimization

Provability & automated business rules (smart contracts).

SAP HANA blockchain

- simplifies access by providing a standard SQL interface

- simplifies the integration into existing SQL-based applications.

- provides a unified API to access various blockchain platforms, allowing a maximum of flexibility.

- replicates data in real-time.

- stores all data in a single storage.

- provides optimized engines to store, analyze and combine these models in a single application.

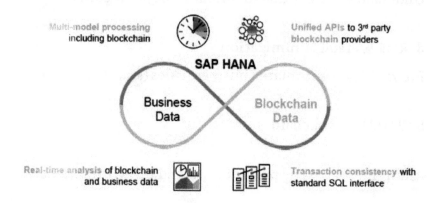

Figure 7.2: Seamless integration of database and blockchain transactions

Image Source: SAP SE / AG

Outcome

Establish trust and transparency across your business network while streamlining processes.

Use Case

Supply chain transparency by extending order processing information to suppliers.

Comprehensive banking analysis through seamless integration of business and blockchain financial transactions.

Blockchain Best Practices

1) Identify the characteristics of the use case

- Does it need to be decentralized?

- Can it work on a central DB + encryption?

- Does it need smart contracts?

- Does it need asset transfer or only verification of assets?

- How much transaction throughput is expected?

- Does it need private transactions?

- Does it need a currency?

2) Ask yourself, is blockchain the right fit?

3) If yes, based on the answers from 1) pick a blockchain technology

4) Determine the Application Pattern

- Simple Document Proof, Provenance tracking, hashing

- Asset transfers

- Business logic in Smart Contracts

5) Determine what data needs to live on chain, and what data can be stored off chain

6) Think about how you would like the accounts (keys) to be managed.

- Local Self-managed

- Local Wallet

- Cloud Wallet

7) Try using established standards and frameworks when writing smart contracts, to avoid security flaws.

NOTES

NOTES

8   CHAPTER 8 – MACHINE LEARNING IN ENTERPRISE APPLICATIONS

SAP Leonardo Machine Learning enables customers and partners to build the intelligent enterprise.

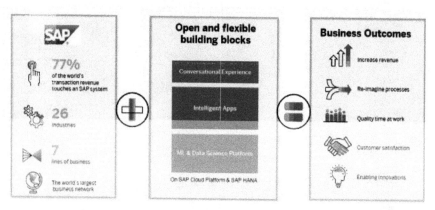

Figure 8.1: How SAP Leonardo ML helps to deliver the Intelligent Enterprise

Image Source: SAP SE / AG

Key Lessons Learnt (kudos to C/4 team)

- Machine Learning (ML) cannot be a "back-box". Explainable AI is key to build trust and make transparent the reasoning behind the prediction

- Clean Data beats More Data & More Data beats Better Algorithms. Focus more on data quality and process maturity then type of algorithm used

- Model is never perfect but it can be useful. Optimize on business goal and trying to minimize loss from model

- Only a small fraction of ML production systems is ML code. Vast majority is for supporting ML and Data infrastructure

- ML in Operations is a way to measure the 'maturity' of business process. Data collected through humans is biased.

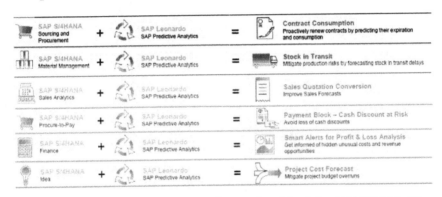

Figure 8.2: SAP Leonardo embedded in S/4HANA Machine Learning and Predictive Analytics

Image Source: SAP SE / AG

SAP Leonardo embedded in S/4HANA Machine Learning helps users in predictive analysis.

SAP S/4HANA	+	SAP Leonardo	=	ML Enabled Business Scenarios
SAP S/4HANA Finance	+	SAP Leonardo SAP Predictive Analytics	=	SAP Business Integrity Screening Increase accuracy of fraud alerts with predictive analytics
SAP S/4HANA Finance	+	SAP Leonardo SAP Predictive Analytics	=	SAP Tax Compliance Smart Automation on Compliance Issue Processing
SAP C/4HANA Cloud 4 Customer	+	SAP Leonardo SAP Predictive Analytics	=	SAP Opportunity Scoring Increase win rates with Predictable sales pipeline and revenue forecast

Figure 8.3: SAP Leonardo intelligent applications

for Machine Learning and Predictive

Image Source: SAP SE / AG

It enables customers and partners to train ML services for their needs.

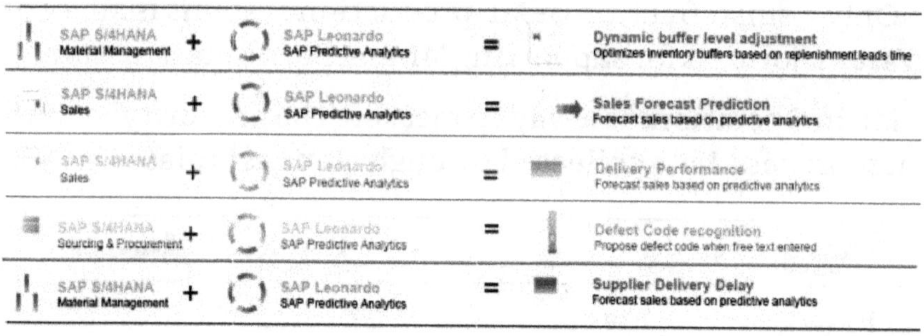

Figure 8.4: SAP Leonardo embedded in S/4HANA Machine Learning and Predictive Analytics

Image Source: SAP SE / AG

NOTES

Sudipta Malakar

NOTES

9   CHAPTER 9 – IMPROVE SAP FIORI ADOPTION WITH SAP BUILD

What is SAP Build?

Build is a comprehensive set of cloud-based tools to quickly develop interactive prototypes, collect user feedback, and jump-start development.

Where does SAP Build Value stand?

- Operationalize design-thinking to spur innovation

- Bring ideas to life through realistic, interactive prototypes with real data

- Improve adoption through early feedback from end-users

- Dramatically reduce development time and cost.

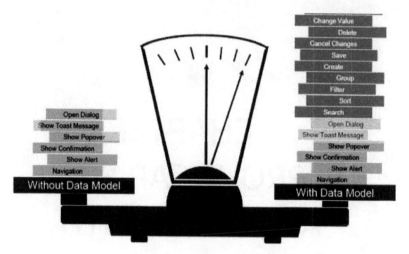

Figure 9.1: UiLogic: The Power of Data

Image Source: SAP SE / AG

"There's no going back, we will always use SAP Build for SAP Fioriapps."

- Robert Blumhof, SVP IT North America, Sika Group

"SAP Build brings excitement to our team and gets to the business case quickly".

- Jo Rose, SAP & Business Systems Manager, Linklaters

NOTES

NOTES

10 CHAPTER 10 – AUTOMATED TESTING WITHIN THE ABAP PROGRAMMING MODEL FOR SAP S/4HANA

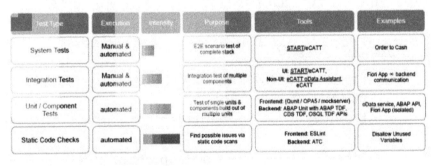

Test Type	Execution	Intensity	Purpose	Tools	Examples
System Tests	Manual & automated		E2E scenario test of complete stack	START/eCATT	Order to Cash
Integration Tests	Manual & automated		Integration test of multiple components	UI: START/eCATT, Non-UI: eCATT oData Assistant, eCATT	Fiori App ≈ backend communication
Unit / Component Tests	automated		Test of single units & components build out of multiple units	Frontend: (Qunit / OPA5 / mockserver) Backend: ABAP Unit with ABAP TDF, CDS TDF, OSQL TDF APIs	oData service, ABAP API, Fiori App (isolated)
Static Code Checks	automated		Find possible issues via static code scans	Frontend: ESLint Backend: ATC	Disallow Unused Variables

Figure 10.1: Recommendation for test automation tools in SAP S/4 HANA

Image Source: SAP SE / AG

Automated unit testing

Unit testing is a software verification and validation method in which a unit (method, function module) of an application will be tested to verify if it satisfies its functional requirements.

GOAL

Unit testing isolates each part of the program and shows that the individual parts work correctly.

UNIT TESTS

- Find problems early in the development cycle

- Help to avoid long debugging sessions

- Make maintenance less painful with automated regression tests

- Provide documentation

- Enables faster software development lifecycle.

ABAP Unit

ABAP unit is the official xUNIT testing framework for ABAP.

FEATURES OF ABAP UNIT

- Provides an environment for execution of unit tests in isolation
- Provides assertion-methods for testing expected results
- Tightly integrated into the programming language ABAP
- Production code and unit test code are bundled and transported together
- Now enhanced to support testing of other development objects like ABAP Core Data Services.

NOTES

Sudipta Malakar

NOTES

11   CHAPTER 11 – TEST YOUR KNOWLEDGE

1. Mention most common challenges faced by your Agile teams.

2. In Agile, is it fair for a customer to ask for expected completion date for a new work item (user story)?

3. Do we accept changes within a sprint, or not? If we do, won't it disrupt our sprint plan that is in progress? And, if we don't, would we be less of an 'agile' team?

4. Mention Kanban myths and misconceptions.

5. Mention Agile myths and misconceptions.

6. What are the common Agile mistakes?

7. What are the common KANBAN mistakes?

8. How do you decide the sprint length for a team?

9. In Agile what are the common estimation techniques?

10. How many planning you are doing in SCRUM?

11. How to reduce technical debt (improving depth of testing, test driven development)?

12. Explain DoR (definition of Ready) and implementation thereof in each sprint?

13. Explain DoD (definition of Done) and implementation thereof in each sprint?

14. Explain UAT before delivery of each sprint in a production environment for integration/testing?

15. Explain "Definition of Ready" (DoR) vs. "Definition of Done" (DoD)?

16. Explain "Agile Estimation and Planning"?

17. Explain critical success factors on PULL mechanism adoption on Agile team rather then PUSH?

18. How team will calculate and optimize Sprint length where 190 team members are working from different geographies' using SCRUM OF SCRUMS?

19. Explain some case studies on successful E2E transformation of Waterfall teams to Agile Teams?

20. Explain some business cases of increasing ROI from business front?

21. Explain common Agile product development Myths?

22. Explain different techniques on backlog prioritization?

23. Explain "Agile Manifesto Myths"?

24. Explain "Turnaround time for a Story"? In Agile, is it fair for a customer to ask for expected

completion date for a new work item (user story)?

25. Should we allow Changes within Sprint?

Do we accept changes within a sprint, or not? If we do, won't it disrupt our sprint plan that is in progress? And, if we don't, would we be less of an 'agile' team?

26. Explain "SAP Activate Methodology" - "Agile way to deliver Cloud based

SAP S/4 HANA Greenfield and Brownfield projects -Creating disruption in 21st Century's Worldwide business Model"?

27. Explain common challenges facing by 1000 members SCRUM of SCRUM teams

working in 5 different Countries?

28. How we can introduce Machine learning and Artificial intelligence in

Agile approach of delivering Projects?

29. How we can introduce blockchain in
Agile approach of delivering Projects?

30. Is PMO role required in Agile Projects?

31. Explain "Less vs. Scrum @Scale vs. Nexus vs. SAFe vs. DAD
in scaling Agile"?

32. Explain RPA (Robotic process automation) in Agile?

33. Explain common Agile mistakes?

34. Explain Yogi requirements from Atlassian?

35. Explain Reiki Practices for Agile Teams?

36. Explain Agile DNA?

37. Explain SPRINT Retrospectives Myths?

38. Explain SPRINT Planning Myths?

39. Explain SPRINT Review Myths?

40. Explain Daily stand-up meeting Myths?

41. Explain different ways to increase SCRUM Teams velocity?

42. Explain challenges in Application platform upgrade in Agile way?

43. Can we measure Productivity of each team member working in SCRUM Project, how?

If not, why?

NOTES

Sudipta Malakar

NOTES

12 CHAPTER 12 – WHERE FOLLOWING AGILE IS NOT APPROPRIATE

Agile is not appropriate for...

- PROJECTS without significant complexity, urgency and uniqueness.

- TEAMS which are not self-organizing and do not believe in inspecting and adapting.

- ORGANIZATIONS which do not invest in good XP practices (e.g. TDD, CI etc.) and cross-functional teams.

- CUSTOMERS who are not willing to be part of the product development team and provide continuous feedback.

- Big Bang – across the board changes without experimentation

- Iterative development without Automated Tests

- Sprints (Iterations) that deliver incomplete work

- Doing mini-waterfalls within the Sprint (Iterations)

- Implementing Agile without believing in its core Values and Principles.

- Projects where scope is almost frozen and doing upfront planning / design

- Projects just "DOING AGILE" rather than "BEING AGILE" mindset

- Projects believing in doing all Customer Projects using 100% automation and following analogous estimation

- Projects using PUSH principles rather than following PULL principles

- Human resources team and Sr. Leadership team do not invest for Agile Certifications / Agile grooming for resources

- Scrum Master follows autonomy and is a dictator

- Product owner fails to create common shared vision in a Team and does not interlock with Business / Customers / Team regularly

NOTES

NOTES

www.ingramcontent.com/pod-product-compliance
Lightning Source LLC
Chambersburg PA
CBHW071402050326
40689CB00010B/1727